Research in Teaching and Learning
Volume 1

PARADIGMS AND PROGRAMS

Lee S. Shulman

A Project of the
AMERICAN EDUCATIONAL RESEARCH
ASSOCIATION

MACMILLAN PUBLISHING COMPANY
A Division of Macmillan, Inc.
NEW YORK

Collier Macmillan Publishers
LONDON

Macmillan Publishing Company
866 Third Avenue, New York, N.Y. 10022
Collier Macmillan Canada, Inc.

Library of Congress Catalog Card Number: 90-33385

Printed in the United States of America

printing number
1   2   3   4   5   6   7   8   9   10

Library of Congress Cataloging-in-Publication Data

Research in teaching and learning : a project of the American
    Educational Research Association.
        p.   cm.
    Chapters from the Handbook of research on teaching.
    Includes bibliographical references.
    Contents: 1. Paradigms and programs / Lee S. Shulman —
2. Quantitative methods / Robert L. Linn. Qualitative methods /
Frederick Erickson — 3. Students' thought processes / Merlin C.
Wittrock. Teachers' thought processes / Christopher M. Clark,
Penelope L. Peterson — 4. Mathematics / Thomas A. Romberg, Thomas
P. Carpenter. Natural sciences / Richard T. White, Richard P.
Tisher.
    1. Education—Research—United States.   2. Teaching.   I. Shulman,
Lee S.   II. American Educational Research Association.
III. Handbook of research on teaching.
LB1028.25.U6R47   1990
370'.7'8073—dc20   90-33385
                                                          CIP

CONTENTS

EDITORIAL NOTE

I want to thank all the people who participated in the creation of the *Handbook of Research on Teaching*. Because of their efforts the *Handbook* continues from its publication in 1986 to receive an overwhelming reception from the world-wide community of researchers and educators interested in the study of teaching.

Because of the exceptional interest in the use of the *Handbook* in the classroom, we have selected several of its chapters for separate publication in the Series *Research in Teaching and Learning*. Each volume of the Series consists of closely related chapters, or of a single chapter, on a theme of particular interest to the readers of the *Handbook*. I hope that the publication of the volumes of this series will further enhance the contributions of the *Handbook of Research on Teaching* to the community of researchers, teachers, and students interested in the study of teaching.

Merlin C. Wittrock
January 30, 1990

Introduction and Overview

This is a chapter about alternatives. It deals with the alternative ways in which the women and men who study teaching go about their tasks. We conduct research in a field to make sense of it, to get smarter about it, perhaps to learn how to perform more adeptly within it. Those who investigate teaching are involved in concerted attempts to understand the phenomena of teaching, to learn how to improve its performance, to discover better ways of preparing individuals who wish to teach. This handbook presents the approaches and results of research on teaching, both to inform readers regarding the current state of theoretical knowledge and practical understanding in the field and to guide future efforts by scholars to add to that fund of understanding.

The purpose of this chapter is to serve as a reader's guide to the field of research on teaching, especially to the research programs that direct, model, or point the ways for research on teaching. The premise behind this chapter is that the field of research on teaching has produced, and will continue to yield, growing bodies of knowledge. But knowledge does not grow naturally or inexorably. It is produced through the inquiries of scholars — empiricists, theorists, practitioners — and is therefore a function of the kinds of questions asked, problems posed, and issues framed by those who do research. To understand the findings and methods of research on teaching, therefore, requires that the reader appreciate the varieties of ways in which such questions are formulated. The framing of a research question, like that of an attorney in a court of law, limits the range of permissible responses and prefigures the character of possible outcomes. Simply put, to interpret the findings of the many studies summarized in this volume, it is essential that the reader understand the questions that have been asked and the manner in which those questions have been framed, both conceptually and methodologically. Research on teaching, like most other fields of study, is not the work of individual scholars working alone and idiosyncratically. Indeed, most research is conducted in the context of scientific communities, "invisible colleges" of

The author thanks reviewers Richard Shavelson (U.C.L.A.) and N. L. Gage (Stanford University) and editorial consultants Walter Doyle and Marianne Amarel for their helpful suggestions.

scholars who share similar conceptions of proper questions, methods, techniques, and forms of explanation. To understand why research is formulated in a particular fashion, one needs to locate the investigation among the alternative approaches to inquiry that characterize a field. A goal of this chapter will be to describe the diverse communities of scholars, practitioners, and policymakers that comprise, or in whose interests are defined, the activities and universe of research on teaching.

The term most frequently employed to describe such research communities, and the conceptions of problem and method they share, is *paradigm.* The term has been used in several ways. In his chapter "Paradigms for Research on Teaching" prepared for the first *Handbook of Research on Teaching* under his editorship, Gage referred to paradigms as "models, patterns, or schemata. Paradigms are not theories; they are rather ways of thinking or patterns for research that, when carried out, can lead to the development of theory" (Gage, 1963, p. 95). Writing during the infancy of this field of research, Gage drew most of his models from psychology or other behavioral sciences, rather than from the study of teaching itself. He was describing how models might be used in the study of teaching, not how they had already been employed. An important sign of the vigor of the field Gage was then fathering is the multiplicity of models from the study of teaching itself that we can now describe some twenty years later. More recently, Doyle (1978; 1983) has written lucidly on the paradigms for research on teaching.

The most famous use of "paradigm" is that of Thomas Kuhn, whose *Structure of Scientific Revolutions* (1970) is a classic of contemporary history of science that has become part of the common parlance and prevailing views of nearly all members of the social and natural science communities. Since one of his friendliest critics (Masterman, 1970) identified some twenty-two different uses of "paradigm" in Kuhn's book, I will refrain from attempting a succinct definition at this point. I prefer to employ the concept of a research program (Lakatos, 1970) to describe the genres of inquiry found in the study of teaching, rather than the Kuhnian conception of a paradigm. Nevertheless, the two terms are used interchangeably in most of the chapter.

The argument of this chapter is that each of the extant research programs grows out of a particular perspective, a bias of either convention or discipline, necessarily illuminating some part of the field of teaching while ignoring the rest. The danger for any field of social science or educational research lies in its potential corruption (or worse, trivialization) by a single paradigmatic view. In this manner, the social sciences and education can be seen as quite different from Kuhn's conception of a mature paradigmatic discipline in the natural sciences, which is ostensibly characterized by a single dominant paradigm whose principles define "normal science" for that field of study.

I will therefore argue that a healthy current trend is the emergence of more complex research designs and research programs that include concern for a wide range of determinants influencing teaching practice and its consequences. These "hybrid" designs, which mix experiment with ethnography, multiple regressions with multiple case studies, process-product designs with analyses of student mediation, surveys with personal diaries, are exciting new developments in the study of teaching. But they present serious dangers as well. They can become utter chaos if not informed by an understanding of the types of knowledge produced by these different approaches. However, the alternative strategy that reduces the richness of teaching to nothing more than the atomism of a multiple variable design may be even worse. This chapter will thus discuss several alternative ways of thinking about "grand strategies" for research on teaching, for programs of research properly construed rather than individual, one-shot investigations.

The chapter will begin with a discussion of the general character of research programs or paradigms, those conceptions of problem and procedure that members of a research community share and in terms of which they pursue their inquiries and exercise their gatekeeping.

After examining the general conception of research programs, a synoptic map of research on the teaching field will be presented. In terms of that map, the various research programs that constitute the field will be described and discussed. This general model will be followed by detailed discussions of the dominant competing (and complementary) research programs currently pursued in the study of teaching.

The next section will discuss the prospects for this field of study, in light of its current progress and present dangers, and in the spirit of contemporary critiques of social science method and theory as exemplified in the work of Cronbach (1975; 1982). Finally, a set of recommendations and anticipations regarding future research programs will be presented. We begin with the matter of research programs or paradigms.

Paradigms and Research Programs

How should teaching be studied? Where does one begin? In what terms can questions be put? Although logically the range and diversity of answers to these questions is vast, in practice, any given scholar appears to operate within a fairly limited repertoire of alternatives. Thus, some researchers always begin with the assumption that their task is to relate, whether experimentally or descriptively, variations in the measured achievement or attitudes of pupils to variations in the observed behavior of teachers. Additional wrinkles may be added to the design — use of individual pupil data as against classroom mean scores, use of pupil- or teacher-characteristic data as mediating variables — but the fundamental character of the questions remains unchanged. Other scholars are equally focused on still other formulations, whether involving classroom discourse, teacher cognitions, the sense pupils make of instruction, or the social organization of classrooms via task or activity structures. Once committed to a particular line of research, the individual scholar seems rarely to stray from it. A research program has been adopted.

Within the terms of such a research program, we can expect that certain kinds of research will be deemed relevant, will be carefully followed and cited by the investigator. A community of like-minded scholars will likely develop, exchanging papers, citing one another's work, using similar language and sharing both assumptions and styles of inquiry. They will agree on the starting points for inquiry. What is problematic? What are sources of wonder or dismay? What are the key topics, the strategic sites, for research? What are the implicit definitions of schooling, of teaching, of learning? What are the units of analysis? What methods of observation and analysis are legitimate? As the answers to such questions evolve, usually without much explicit debate, a kind of paradigm may be inferred to have developed.

A word on paradigms is in order. The concept of a paradigm became part of the working vocabulary of social scientists under the influence of Thomas Kuhn (1970). In Kuhn's sense of the term, a paradigm is an implicit, unvoiced, and pervasive commitment by a community of scholars to a conceptual framework. In a mature science, only one paradigm can be dominant at a time. It is shared by that community, and serves to define proper ways of asking questions, those common "puzzles" that are defined as the tasks for research in normal science. Members of the community acknowledge and incorporate the work of perceived peers in their endeavors. Kuhn would expect members of such a group to be relatively incapable of communicating meaningfully with members of other communities. (Quite literally, the ability to *communicate* is a central definer of *community* membership.) Moreover, they would have difficulty comprehending why members of another paradigmatic community would find the particular puzzles they pursue of either importance or value.

A research program not only defines what can be legitimately studied by its advocates, it also specifies what is necessarily excluded from the list of permissible topics. For example, in their landmark *The Study of Teaching*, Dunkin and Biddle (1974) explicitly exclude certain kinds of research from their review. In doing so, they leave out all studies that do not employ quantifiable measures of process or product. Ironically, the work of Jackson (1968) in *Life in Classrooms* is explicitly left out of consideration, even though it is among the most frequently cited references in their conceptual analysis of teaching.

In examining the effects of paradigms on the activities of researchers, we should distinguish between two general ways in which the term can be employed. The first sense, that which Kuhn intended in his characterization of the history of physics and other natural sciences, limits a discipline to but a single dominant paradigm during any particular epoch. He reports (Kuhn, 1970, pp. vii–viii) that he was drawn to that view during a year spent at the Center for Advanced Study in the Behavioral Sciences when, for the first time, he found himself in extended colleagueship with a community of social scientists. He observed that they seemed to argue, even when from the same discipline, about basic matters of theory and method that physical scientists tended to take for granted. It was then he realized that they failed to share a common conception of their fields so characteristic of the more "mature" disciplines. He called that network of shared assumptions and conceptions a paradigm, and concluded that the social sciences were, therefore, "pre-paradigmatic" in their development.

There is a second, weaker sense of paradigm I prefer to use in this chapter. Social scientists pursue their research activities within the framework of a school of thought that defines proper goals, starting points, methods, and interpretive conceptions for investigations (see Schwab, 1960/1978). These schools of thought operate much like Kuhnian paradigms or Lakatosian research programs insofar as they are relatively insular and predictably uniform. However, in no sense are social science fields necessarily dominated by a single school of thought. Indeed, as Kuhn observed, what distinguishes the social from the natural sciences is this very absence of a single dominant paradigm.

Where Kuhn erred, I believe, is in diagnosing this characteristic of the social sciences as a developmental disability, a state of preparadigmatic retardation. Indeed, it is far more likely that for the social sciences and education, the coexistence of competing schools of thought is a natural and quite mature state. In this matter, I agree fully with Merton's observations about sociology:

> The chronic crisis of sociology, with its diversity, competition and clash of doctrine, seems preferable to the ... prescription of a single theoretical perspective that promises to provide full and exclusive access to the sociological truth. ... No one paradigm has even begun to demonstrate its unique cogency for investigating the entire range of sociologically interesting questions. And given the variety of these questions, the past prefigures the future. (Merton, 1975, p. 28)

Merton argues for the superiority of a set of competing paradigms over the hegemony of a single school of thought. He asserts that theoretical pluralism encourages development of a variety of research strategies, rather than premature closure of investigation consistent with the problematics of a single paradigm. Different paradigms alert research workers to different phenomena of interest, different conceptions of problem, and different aspects of events likely to be ignored within a single perspective. He advocates the virtues of "a plurality of theoretical orientations ... in the form of a 'disciplined eclecticism'" (ibid., p. 51).

> The cognitive problems of coexisting paradigms call for discovering the capabilities and limitations of each. This involves identifying the kinds and range of problems each is good for (and noting those for

which it is incompetent or irrelevant), thus providing for potential awareness of the respects in which they are complementary or contradictory. ... Many ideas in structural analysis and symbolic interactionism, for example, are opposed to one another in about the same sense as ham is opposed to eggs: they are perceptibly different but mutually enriching. (Merton, 1975, pp. 50, 31)

The philosopher of science Feyerabend (1974) puts the matter even more directly in his essay "How to Be a Good Empiricist: A Plea for Tolerance in Matters Epistemological":

You can be a good empiricist only if you are prepared to work with many alternative theories rather than with a single point of view and "experience." This plurality of theories must not be regarded as a preliminary stage of knowledge which will at some time in the future be replaced by the One True Theory. (p. 14)

This is also the view of the present chapter regarding the proper treatment of the alternative research programs to be discussed presently.

Gage (1963) presented a comprehensive review of paradigms for research on teaching in the first *Handbook of Research on Teaching*, compiled under his editorship. He reviewed a host of exemplars of paradigms from other social sciences that might prove valuable for studies of teaching, then proceeded to explore those that had been used for research on classroom teaching itself. By far the most influential source of paradigms for the study of teaching came from psychology, especially the behavioristic, experimental, functional perspective within that discipline. He defined "criterion-of-effectiveness" paradigms that specified criteria for judging the success with which a teacher had performed his or her tasks and related that criterion to a variety of potential correlates to discern those that were most consistently and powerfully associated with achievement of the criterion.

Potential Correlates → Criterion of Effectiveness

Gage distinguished among several types of effectiveness criteria (and microcriteria, specific outcome variables rather than general ones) as well as types of design. He then discussed "teaching process" paradigms, where the emphasis of the research was on characterizing the observable teacher and student behaviors in the classroom as they related to measures of pupil growth. Summarizing across the several models of teaching process research, he found four common elements. These were (a) the perceptual and cognitive processes of the teacher, which eventuate in (b) action elements on the teacher's part. The teacher's actions are followed by (c) perceptual and cognitive processes on the pupil's part, which in turn lead to (d) actions on the part of pupils (Gage, 1963, p. 127).

It is somewhat ironic that in this important and early characterization of research paradigms, the cognitive and affective internal states of both learners and teachers are given equal weight with the observable actions of each. As the field continued to develop, the interest in those perceptual and cognitive states that are hypothesized to produce and mediate observable behavior waned. The dominant research program for the study of teaching combined a microcriterion of effectiveness (tested academic achievement) and teaching process correlates.

Gage recognized the limitations of these paradigms. He commented on the importance of classrooms as places where teachers must deal with more than one pupil at a time, a fact often ignored by then-extant models. He also observed that the unit of interaction connoted by those paradigms was typically the "single interact," ignoring the larger and more complex exchanges that constituted the important features of classroom process. On the other hand, it was important to begin the enormously difficult job of studying classroom behavior, and a number of simplifications were necessary. Those simplifications were provided by the early models and made possible the important first steps in the development of the field.

Some 10 years later, in *The Study of Teaching*, Dunkin and Biddle (1974) constructed a model for research on teaching based on an earlier formulation by Mitzel (1960). They posited four classes of variables: presage variables (teacher characteristics, experiences, training, and other properties that influence teaching behavior), context variables (properties of pupils, of the school and community, and of the classroom), process variables (observable actions of teachers and students in the classroom), and product variables (immediate and long-term effects of teaching on pupil growth intellectually, socially, emotionally, and the like).While it is unfair to characterize such a sophisticated and prescient work too simply, their formulation had an

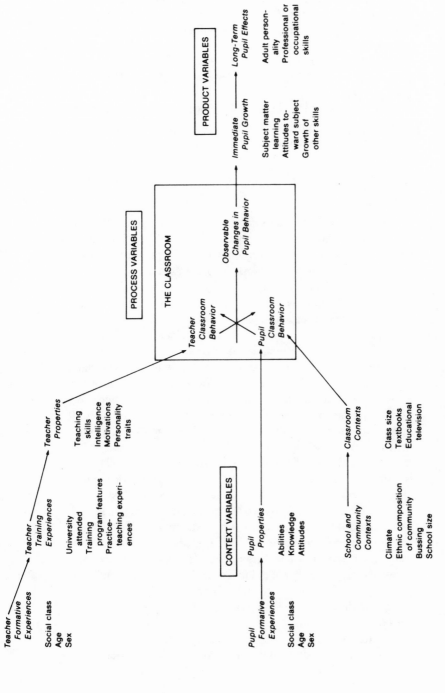

Fig. I. A model for the study of classroom teaching. From *The study of teaching* (New York: Holt, Rinehart, and Winston) by M. J. Dunkin and B. J. Biddle, 1974. Reprinted by permission.

9

enormous impact on the field. The emphasis on studies relating processes to products did not begin with their reviews. But their book gave strong impetus to the process-product work and helped embed it in a more comprehensive theoretical matrix. Moreover, they provided the working vocabulary for those who followed to describe what they were studying and how they were going about it.

The next section shall present a more general model for research on teaching, reflecting changes in the field, both observed and needed, during the last decade.

A Synoptic Map of Research on Teaching

In asserting that no single research program can capture the full set of educational events, I imply that the insufficiencies of particular programs can be overcome through proper blending with the insufficiencies of other programs. This image of a yoking of inadequacies to produce a hybrid more vigorous than either of its parents is certainly not alien to the practice of agriculture, but it has not been widely touted in the social sciences.

Two matters can be mentioned at this juncture. First, while most disciplines or fields of study become identified with narrowly defined methods, others have developed traditions of eclecticism, a penchant for employing a variety of methods for both acquiring information and subjecting it to analysis and interpretation. Among the traditional disciplines, most prominent is history, whose activities are so diversely puzzling to many outsiders that there is often debate over whether history is more properly classified among the social sciences or the humanities. Yet it is, I shall argue, precisely because history so readily defies categorization (or so comfortably accepts multiple affiliation) that it may serve as a useful analogy for the kind of multiple paradigmatic inquiry I shall advocate in this chapter. Moreover, it manages its several faces while surviving as both a form of fundamental investigation and as a significant source of guidance for both policy and practice — at least for those who do not choose to ignore it.

I begin with the assumption that there is no "real world" of the classroom, of learning and of teaching. There are many such worlds, perhaps nested within one another, perhaps occupying parallel universes which frequently, albeit unpredictably, intrude on one another. Each of these worlds is occupied by the same people, but in different roles and striving for different purposes simultaneously. Each of these contexts is studied by social scientists and educators, becoming the subject of theoretical models and treatises. Each has its own set of concepts and principles and, quite inevitably, its own set of facts, for facts are merely those particular phenomena to which our questions and principles direct our attention.

We become involved in these different worlds as elements of our puzzle because we most often must make a particular level or strand the subject of empirical study, but then we attempt to infer properties of other strands from the one we have investigated. Thus, for example, we conduct studies of how individual students learn to perform certain complex school tasks, and then infer principles for the learning of similar tasks by groups of students. Similarly, we may study classrooms of youngsters and then use the data to recommend policy for a school or school district. The essence of the puzzle lies in recognizing that no benevolent deity has ordained that these parallel lives be consistent with one another, nor that the principles found to work at one level must operate similarly at others.

Indeed, I would contend that our most reasonable hypothesis is that each of these lives must be studied in its own terms. We must attempt to capture the essential features of each strand in one or more middle-range theories (Merton, 1967) which render accounts of the teaching–learning episodes that characterize that level. These episodes provide the dramatic material for lives in that context, and define the strategic research sites (Merton, 1959) within which we make theoretical sense of what occurs there. Since those strategic research sites are different in each strand, so must be the strategic investigations, hence the facts, principles, and theories that emerge from those investigations. It is unlikely that any single theoretical frame can encompass the diversity of sites, events, facts, and principles that cross all those levels.

Any claim that the worlds of teaching, of schools and classrooms, of pedagogues and pupils, are so complex that no single perspective can capture them should be treated with skepticism. Like our suspicions of the mythical sociologist who asserts that all generalizations are false, we must ask how the claim can be made. It is fashionable to recall the ancient image of the blind men who provide alternative portrayals of an elephant whose unseen bulk is not perceptible to any one of them. Yet that tale presupposes the talents of a sighted observer who possesses knowledge of the total pachyderm and can thus grasp the futility of each assessment from the blind inquirers. Likewise in a field of scholarship, the observer who claims to possess precisely the kind of knowledge that he asserts is, in principle, unavailable to his fellows makes a claim we must find suspect. For those who conduct research on teaching are not blind, and relative to my fellow scholars I can claim no special gift of insight.

Given that my rationality is as limited as anyone else's, I have attempted to piece together a more comprehensive portrayal of the field through incorporating reports arriving from many vantage points (or touching points, in the case of our metaphor). By combining these separate accounts of teaching from different families of researchers, accounts much like the tales of early mariners regarding the geographic wonders they encountered on their journeys, we can begin to fashion a broader picture of our phenomena.

This map, however, cannot be a comprehensive *theory* of teaching. It is a representation of the variety of topics, programs, and findings of the field of research on teaching, related to one another as usefully as possible. For it to be useful, we must attempt to construct a map of the full domain of research on teaching (or several alternative maps, each highlighting different features, analogous to political subdivisions, the physical features and elevations, climatic conditions, and the like), a map sufficiently broad and encompassing that we can locate upon it not only the particular sections of terrain well captured by particular programs but also those left out. Moreover, we must seek to construct maps that themselves have some coherence or order, so our analyses can go beyond a mere shopping list of topics *qua* ingredients, some of which just happen to be omitted from any one particular treatment.

The fundamental terms in my analysis are the primary participants — teacher(s) and student(s) — who may be studied as individuals or as members of a larger group, class, or school. Teaching is seen as an activity involving teachers and students working jointly. The work involves the exercise of both thinking and acting on the parts of all participants. Moreover, teachers learn and learners teach. Both those functions of each actor can be considered an essential part of the inquiry.

The potential determinants of teaching and learning in the classroom are the three significant attributes of the actors — capacities, actions, and thoughts. *Capacities* are the relatively stable and enduring characteristics of ability, propensity, knowledge, or character inhering in the actors, yet capable of change through either learning or development. *Actions* comprise the activities, performances, or behavior of actors, the observable physical or speech acts of teachers and students. *Thoughts* are the cognitions, metacognitions, emotions, purposes — the tacit mental and emotional states that precede, accompany, and follow the observable actions, frequently foreshadowing (or reflecting) changes in the more enduring capacities. Both thoughts and behavior can become capacities (in the form, for example, of knowledge and habits or skills).

The activities of teaching can take place in a number of contexts, "surrounds" which define, in part, the milieu in which teaching occurs — individual, group, class, school, community. Within each of these nested levels (See Barr & Dreeben, 1983a; 1983b), the two sorts of transactions that comprise classroom life are occurring. Two sorts of agendas are being followed, two sorts of curriculum are being negotiated. One agenda is the organizational, interactional, social, and management aspect of classroom life, sometimes dubbed the hidden curriculum, though its visibility has improved dramatically as it has been studied. The second band of transmission is the academic task, school assignment, classroom content, and manifest curriculum. The contents of these two agendas, these forms of pedagogical transmission, are at the very heart of the educational enterprise, because they define what schools are for, what purposes they are designed to accomplish. The dual general purposes of transmitting mastery of the contents of a curriculum, comprising many subjects, skills, and attitudes, and of socializing a generation of young people through the workings of the classroom community define the core of classroom life.

Since the events we are coming to understand occur in classrooms and schools, they invariably occur in the service of teaching *something*. That something is usually capable of characterization as the content of a subject (e.g., Shakespeare's *Hamlet*, quadratic equations, diagraming sentences, word-attack skills, Boyle's Law), a particular set of skills, strategies, processes or understandings relative to the subject matter, or a set of socialization outcomes. The content ought not be viewed as only a "context variable" (Dunkin & Biddle, 1974), comparable to class size or classroom climate. The content and the purposes for which it is taught are the very heart of the teaching–learning processes. Smith (1983) put it clearly when he asserted that the "teacher interacts with the student in and through the content, and the student interacts with the teacher in the same way" (p. 491). Although the content transmitted for particular purposes has rarely been a central part of studies of teaching, it certainly deserves a place in our comprehensive map, if only to remind us of its neglect.

Central to any discussion of content is the unit of instructional activity that serves as the starting point for analyses of teaching. Is it the individual interchange between student(s) and teacher, the episode (e.g., quelling a particular behavioral disturbance, or explaining a new concept), the lesson (say, a 20-minute reading group session), the unit (e.g., a six-day sequence on the Age of Jackson in a U.S. history course), the semester course, or the year of work? If it is a longer analytic unit, is it assumed to be decomposable into an aggregation of discrete interchanges or episodes, or is it dealt with as a totality in itself? These are certainly critical choices for the researcher. In addition, conceptions of content itself are important. These include those deriving from philosophers of education (e.g., the distinction between substantive and syntactic structures [Schwab, 1962/1978]), from instructional psychologists (e.g., facts, concepts, principles, cognitive strategies), or from cognitive psychologists (schemata, scripts, metacognitions, etc.).

Finally, the perspective taken by the research can be that of an outside observer attempting to discover the lawful relationships among the observable features, or the emphasis can be on discovering the meanings constructed by the participants as they attempt to make sense of the circumstances they both encounter and create. These two aspects are sometimes called the positivistic and the interpretive, or the *etic* and the *emic* (following the tradition in linguistics of distinguishing between phon*etic* and phon*emic* analyses).

The drawing of Figure 2 attempts to portray the relationships among these units of inquiry. Almost all research on teaching examines the relationships among features, be they capacities, actions, or thoughts as evidenced by the participants conceptualized in some fashion. Research programs differ in the

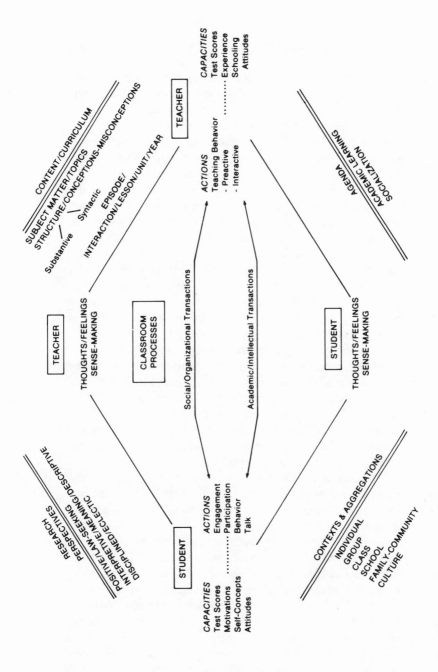

Fig. 2. Synoptic map of research on teaching.

15

particular features chosen for analysis, the direction of causality implied by the discussion (e.g., teacher → student; students → teacher; students ↔ teacher, reflexively or interactively caused joint behavior of students and teacher), the agendas to which they attend, the level of aggregation or context at which relationships are sought, and the perspective taken with respect to the activities or experiences of the participants.

Thus, for example, research in the tradition of teacher characteristics typically examined the relationships between indicators of teacher capacities (e.g., teacher test scores, years of experience, personality measures) and of student capacities (e.g., achievement test scores, attitudes toward self or school). At other times, teacher capacities were related to student actions (e.g., student ratings of course satisfaction).

The process–product tradition studies the relationships of teaching performance and subsequent student capacities. The Academic Learning Time program relates teaching performance to student actions, as inferred from the time allocations made by students. The student mediation program focuses on student thoughts and feelings, usually in relation to teacher actions and subsequent student actions or capacities. The teacher cognition program examines the relationships of teacher thought to teacher action (e.g., studies of judgment policies and teachers' assignments of pupils to reading groups). The classroom ecology program examines the reflexive influences of teacher and student actions, frequently illuminated by aspects of thought. Different patterns of interaction may subsequently be related to changes in students' capacities.

The study of teaching usually involves coming to understand the relationships, in the forms of causes or reasons, among these different aspects of teaching and learning. But such a model alone does not portray those research efforts. Different research programs for the study of teaching select different parts of the map to define the phenomena for their inquiries. There are also other sorts of choices that determine the manner in which research on teaching is conducted. These include predilections for qualitative as against quantitative research methods, disciplinary or interdisciplinary orientation, preference for the characterization of behavior as against the representation of thought — behaviorism versus mentalism, to use somewhat older terms — and, most broadly, the conception of one's craft as a science in search of laws or as an exercise of interpretation in search or meanings.

The Major Research Programs

In the sections that follow, the major research programs that organize the bulk of research on teaching will be presented, described, analyzed, contrasted, and criticized. It will not be the purpose of this chapter to review the literature of each program, or even to summarize its central findings fully. Indeed, the many chapters which follow in this handbook are devoted to this demanding task. As each program is presented, I shall attempt to outline its central organizing questions, the topics and paths in the synoptic model it occupies, the prototypical designs and methods it employs, and the types of findings it generates.

I shall emphasize in particular the manner in which research programs have developed in response and reaction to other programs. Quite typically, new research programs did not develop as alternative ways to accomplish the research objectives of existing programs. Instead, investigators reacted against particular aspects of an existing program — the report of findings that were not believable, the extrapolation to policies that were ideologically or politically unacceptable, the use of methods that were considered questionable. This conception of the research-on-teaching field as a Great Conversation, an ongoing dialogue among investigators committed to understanding and improving teaching, is central to the discussion that follows.

We will begin with the central and most active program in research on teaching, process–product research, followed by its close cousin, albeit occasional critic, the program of research on academic learning time. We will see how the student mediation program occupies a position midway between the perspectives of process–product research and studies of classroom processes as ecological systems or as language communities. The study of teacher cognition will be examined in parallel to examinations of pupil cognition in several programs. We turn first to process–product research.

Process–Product Research

Easily the most vigorous and productive of the programs of research on teaching during the past decade has been the teaching effectiveness approach, also known as the process–product program in the terminology of Mitzel (1960) and of Dunkin and Biddle (1974). Its key contributors have been Gage (1978), Soar (e.g., Soar & Soar, 1979), Brophy (e.g., 1983), Evertson,

Emmer (e.g., Evertson, Emmer, Sanford, & Clements, 1983), Bennett (e.g., Bennett, Jordan, Long, & Wade, 1976), Good (e.g., 1979), Stallings (e.g., Stallings & Kaskowitz, 1974), Kounin (e.g., 1970), and others, with periodic review papers by Rosenshine (e.g., 1983) serving to consolidate the body of work into conceptions of direct instruction or, more recently, active teaching (Good, Grouws, & Ebmeier, 1983). Work in this program is reviewed by Brophy and Good, Good and Brophy, and by Rosenshine and Stevens, all in this volume. Those studies dealing predominantly with classroom management are discussed by Doyle, also in this volume. The basic tenets of process-product research were described by Anderson, Evertson, and Brophy (1979)

> ... to define relationships between what teachers do in the classroom (the processes of teaching) and what happens to their students (the products of learning). One product that has received much attention is achievement in the basic skills. ... Research in this tradition assumes that greater knowledge of such relationships will lead to improved instruction: once effective instruction is described, then supposedly programs can be designed to promote those effective practices. (p. 193)

In a similar fashion, McDonald and Elias (1976) observed:

> A major goal was to estimate the effects of teachers' actions or teaching performances on pupil learning. The assumption was made that differences among teachers in how they organize instruction, in the methods and materials they use, and in how they interact with pupils would have different effects on how much children learned. ... The major analyses of this study were of the relations of the scores representing differences in teaching performances to differences in pupil learning. (p. 6)

The teaching effectiveness studies are typically conducted in existing classrooms that function normally during the periods of observation (the term "naturalistic" is used, though "natural" is a more accurate description.) Observers ordinarily use categorical observation scales, typically of the "low inference" variety (tallying the occurrence of observable events rather than judging or evaluating the quality of observed activities, which would be deemed "high inference") and most often spread a set of observation occasions (as few as four to as many as twenty) across most of the school year.

The units of analysis are generally the school day (or whatever portion of the day constituted the observation period) and the actions of the teacher and students. These actions can be treated alone (frequency of teacher asking higher-order questions; incidence of calling on pupils in a predetermined order) or as chains or sequences of teacher action → pupil response → teacher reaction (e.g., higher-order question → correct pupil response of particular sort → teacher praise). The subsequent analyses nearly always disaggregate the observed classroom processes into the categories employed in the observation instrument (or composites constructed subsequently) and then combine those observations across observational days and across all teachers observed. Thus, incidents of teacher questioning or praise in Classroom A will be aggregated across all n days of observation in that classroom to investigate the effectiveness of such questioning, as well as combine with the results for such questioning observed in all other teachers.

In contrast to some other research programs, the effectiveness of teaching is seen as attributable to combinations of discrete and observable teaching performances per se, operating relatively independent of time and place. Scholars in this tradition regularly speak of controlling for "context variables." These are usually fairly static categories like subject matter, age and sex of students, ability levels of students, type of school, and so forth. Data from early in an observational hour are combined with data from late on the same occasion. Data from fall may be combined with data from spring. Data from a unit on natural selection combines with data from a unit on the circulation of the blood. All these are seen as instances of teaching, an activity that transcends both individual teachers and specific situations.

It is not surprising that one of the leading figures in this tradition, N. L. Gage (1978), advocates the "meta-analysis" of research findings from process–product studies to discover more stable relationships between teaching behavior and pupil performance. In quest for a mode of analysis that would provide better-grounded inferences regarding the relationships of teaching and achievement than can be gleaned from single studies examined individually, he urges

> ... converting the exact probability value of the result of any single study into a value of the statistic called chi square. Then the values

of chi square are summed over studies, and the significance, or probability, of the sum is determined. In essence, the technique provides an estimate of the statistical significance, or "non-chanceness,"of the whole cluster of independent findings that are considered by the research reviewer to deal with a specified process variable, or aspect of teacher behavior or teaching method. (Gage, 1978, p. 29)

Meta-analysis thus serves as the cross-investigation equivalent of the logic of process–product research itself. We are urged to sum statistics across studies, just as we have summed the values of individual teachers' behavior across both situations and the observed behavior of other teachers. There is assumed to be an underlying "true score" for the relationship between a given teacher behavior and a pupil outcome measure. There is a parameter or law which can be estimated. The problem is to get beyond the limitations of particular teachers, particular classrooms, particular studies to a more stable generalization.

What accounts for the vigor of the process-product research program? Why have its central constructs — teacher effectiveness, direct instruction, active teaching, time-on-task — been so readily accepted and applied by practitioners and policy makers? After many decades during which the study of teaching and learning *in vivo* (rather than in the laboratory) was either pursued only by evaluators (e.g., the classroom observations of the Eight-Year Study) or essentially ignored, why did it rise phoenix-like from the ashes of educational research? But why, especially, has this particular school of thought gained such dominance in the field?

The process–product research program has had many virtues. First, the approach was responsive to the important topics being discussed in the Great Conversation. Within educational policy circles, the Coleman Report (Coleman, et al., 1966) had created a sensation, especially with its apparent claim that teachers, or more accurately variations among teachers, do not make a difference in school achievement. But Coleman's findings were based on a classic input–output production function analysis of schools and included no data on the actual teaching events of classroom life. A number of classroom researchers (whose work was summarized by Good, Biddle, & Brophy, 1975) were motivated to study teacher effectiveness to provide a more stringent test of Coleman's assertion. One of the most significant sets of findings from process-product research on teaching entailed the demonstration that teachers *did* make a difference. Variations in teacher behavior were found to be systematically related to variations in student achievement, a finding that was only possible from a research design relating teaching *processes* to student *products*.

Another central topic in the late 60s was teacher expectations, an interest that resulted from the publication of the provocative and controversial study *Pygmalion in the Classroom* (Rosenthal & Jacobson 1968). Without directly documenting teacher behavior, the authors claimed that teachers were subtly communicating their expectations to pupils through patterns of praise, questioning, tones of voice, and opportunities to learn. Was there really an expectation effect? Did teachers act differently toward students for whom they held different expectations? Toward children of different gender or race? Were such differences, if detected, related systematically to variations in student performance? These types of research questions demanded meticulous descriptions of teacher behavior in relation to individual students. In turn, those descriptions could be related to student characteristics and to eventual student achievement as well. They were a significant impetus for the development of process-product research (Brophy & Good, 1974). Thus, this form of research first gained credence because of its value in dealing with major questions addressed by educators in relation to the effectiveness of teachers and the power of their expectations.

Second, process-product research was consistent with a strong existing research tradition — applied behavioristic psychology and its task-analytic, training tradition wherein the decomposition of complex tasks into their components followed by the assessment and retraining of individuals on the components themselves had a demonstrably successful track record (e.g., Glaser, 1962; Gagné, 1970). If the decomposition of a complex skill worked for radar technicians, aircraft mechanics, second-language learners, and other skilled performers, why not for teachers? The metaphor of teaching as skill, or bundle of skills, deployed across variations in setting, was both compelling and well understood within the educational research and practice communities.

Third, unlike the laboratory tradition for the study of learning, this program of research was carried out in naturally occurring classrooms. The teachers who were observed were performing normally, carrying out their duties in the natural context of instruction. Therefore, the generalizations about teaching effectiveness were not based on a "test-tube" classroom, but on the real thing. It would be impossible to claim that the findings could not be applied because such behavior was impractical. Indeed, the behavior has already been observed in typical classrooms with enough frequency to have been identified as effective or ineffective.

Fourth, the implications of the research program for practice and policy were frequently seen as straightforward. Those who read the research often saw it as having clear implications for practice and policy. The research frequently identifies large numbers of teacher behaviors, discrete variables that were correlated with student outcomes and that defined the key elements of teaching effectiveness. These, in turn, lent themselves to lists of "teachers should" statements that were handy to those who wished to prescribe or mandate specific teaching policies for the improvement of schools. Moreover, the work was tied to an indicator that both policy makers and laypersons took most seriously as a sign of how schoolchildren were doing: standardized achievement tests.

The sign rapidly evolved into the signified, the indicator into the end in itself. The raising of test scores became a goal of instruction. Teaching performances that were observable could both be evaluated and serve as the basis for training and staff development. The competency-based teacher education movement flourished energetically for several years, and though on the wane in schools of education is reemerging at the state level in programs for beginning teachers and/or for evaluating teachers for certification, tenure, or merit increases. This dual advantage of ready association with observable results for pupils and the appearance of clear implications for evaluation, training, and policy, made the process–product approach attractive indeed. Although a number of process–product researchers actively opposed the oversimplification of their findings, warning against the premature application of results, others seemed to encourage the development of teacher education or evaluation systems that employed the findings of their studies as a framework for assessing teacher quality. Process–product researchers were surely not alone in seeing their work so used. The work on Academic Learning Time lent itself even more readily to naive misuse by policy makers, whose prescriptions of "more time-on-task," longer school days, and extended school years would typically cite research as the basis for their recommendations.

Finally, the approach worked. The studies conducted under its programmatic direction accomplished the sorts of important aims outlined for them. Teachers who consistently were associated with higher achievement gains tended to behave differently from those who were not. The data accumulated across correlational studies and survived experimental field tests. Teachers seemed capable of learning to perform in the manners suggested by the research program and the performances tended to produce higher achievement among their pupils. Within the limits of whatever activities standardized achievement tests were measuring, the program was palpably successful. Not only were the proposed interventions effective, they were typically acceptable and credible to experienced teachers. The dictates of direct instruction or the principles of active teaching made sense to most teachers, at least to those not ideologically wedded to images of open classrooms and progressive education. Along with conceptions of "time-on-task" and the heavy emphasis on strong teacher control and management, the program produced scientific support for approaches to instruction with which the majority of teachers, administrators, and parents felt intuitively and professionally comfortable.

The timing of the research program was also fortunate, coming as it did during the national reaction against the laissez-faire character of the youth culture during the late 1960s and early 1970s. The concern over test-score declines, adolescent misbehavior, and poor school discipline produced an emphasis on a return to the basics, both in behavior and in curriculum. The educational climate was ripe for a return to traditional values — back to basics, to discipline, to phonetics, to computation, to penmanship, to homework, to teachers in charge of kids, and principals in charge of their schools, to less down-time and more time-on-task   in short, back to an image of schooling in which there was less question about who was in charge and what was to be learned.

The contrast to the late 1950s is fascinating, for although the threat of Russian science was a significant goad to national educational and curriculum reform, the emphasis on beefing up the subject matter was matched with strong concern for inquiry, discovery, and problem solving, for student-initiated activities and divergent thinking, for ascending the heights of Bloom's taxonomy. The opinion leaders were less concerned with the basics than with those more elevated understandings that are needed to be scientifically literate and competitive. The process-product work conducted at the time, Flanders's (1970) pioneering efforts studying classroom interaction with categorical observation instruments, did not lead to the conclusion that direct instruction was best. In fact, Flanders had concluded that "indirect teaching" was the most effective approach to classroom instruction.

(An interesting footnote may be added here. Barr and Dreeben (1978) reanalyzed Flanders's tables because of the apparent contradiction between his earlier findings and those of the process-product researchers of the 1970s. While this discrepancy could certainly have been another example of Cronbach's (1975) "decade-by-treatment interactions," a simpler explanation was offered. Flanders defined his "indirect teaching" score as a ratio between indirect and direct teaching. Barr and Dreeben found that those teachers who had the highest ratio also displayed the largest *amount* of teaching overall. They not only did more indirect teaching. They simply did more teaching. Therefore, the apparent contradiction melted away.)

The major findings from the teaching effectiveness literature produced in the process-product program are summarized by Brophy and Good (Handbook Ch. 12). The program of research contains many variants. Most of the research is descriptive and correlational, with several field experiments in recent years. In some cases, teachers are preselected as unusually effective based on analysis of their class achievements during the previous one to three years. In other cases, effectiveness is measured only after the fact by the performance of students at the end of the year, and then retrospectively correlated with each of the observational categories. In some cases, the frequency of types of teacher behavior is tallied without regard to the particular pupils who were targets for the behavior. In other studies, differences in the behavior of the same teacher vis-à-vis individual pupils are examined.

Overall, the findings take the form of propositions describing those forms of teacher behavior that are associated with gains in student performance, often conditioned on grade level and subject matter. That aspect of teacher behavior usually described is either classroom management behavior (responses to misbehavior, allocating of turns, establishment of rules) or generic instructional behavior (use of lower- or higher-order questions, frequency of praise or criticism [treated as feedback], wait-time), rather than behavior describing the *substantive* subject-specific content of instruction (e.g., choice of examples, sources of metaphors, type of subtraction algorithm employed, reading comprehension strategy demonstrated and explained, and the like).

As time passes, the process–product program seems surprisingly to be losing intellectual vigor within the research community. Though at the levels of practice and policy it remains the most widely used and cited body of work (exemplified especially by the impressive studies of direct instruction or active classroom teaching, e.g., Good, Grouws, & Ebmeier, 1983, and those of classroom management, e.g., Emmer, Evertson, & Anderson, 1980), the other research programs to be described in this chapter have gained the interest and investment of the newer generation of scholars on teaching. Why has this been the case?

There are several reasons to consider. First, the program has succeeded relative to its own goals. So often when a program succeeds, that very success leads critics to consider goals beyond those envisaged by the program and to criticize the program for failing to accomplish them. The program's leaders understandably respond with great frustration, since their success in accomplishing their proposed goals is inadequately acknowledged when the criticisms grow most strident. Moreover, the funds needed to conduct large-scale process–product research have diminished considerably.

Second, while the claim could be made that the program studied naturally occurring behavior and therefore met the ultimate reality tests, in principle, the manner in which individual behavioral elements were aggregated into patterns or styles of teaching performance did not necessarily meet this criterion. Gage (1978), explains the distinction between styles as naturally occurring patterns and styles as composites in the following passage:

> Before we proceed, we should note the difference between two methods of research. The first compares intact patterns of teaching, such

as direct and open styles. This method studies the relationship between these patterns of teaching and what pupils learn. The second method deals with many specific dimensions, or variables, of teaching styles or methods. Here the investigators study the relationships between each of hundreds of variables within various teaching styles and what pupils learn. *From the hundreds of correlations, especially the significant ones, the investigators and reviewers then synthesize the style or pattern of teaching that seems to be associated with desirable kinds of pupil achievement and attitude.* (p. 31; italics added).

Thus the bulk of process-product research, while based on naturally occurring correlations, defined effective teaching through an act of synthesis by the investigator or reviewer, in which the individual behaviors associated with desirable pupil performance were aggregated into a new composite. There was little evidence that any observed teacher had ever performed in the classroom congruent with the collective pattern of the composite.

A most important development in this program was the series of field experiments in which the composites were translated into experimental teacher training treatments. Studies such as Anderson, Evertson and Brophy (1979), or Good, Grouws, and Ebmeier (1983), as summarized and interpreted by Gage and Giaconia (1981), and Gage (in press) reported on naturalistic field experiments in which teachers who had been trained using the composites typically produced higher achievement gains among their students than did their control counterparts. Even in these cases, however, it was typically found that the teachers in the experimental treatments did not always engage in the "desired" behaviors more frequently than did their control counterparts. Moreover, not all the trained behaviors continued to correlate with the student achievement criteria in the field experiments. This further suggests that all the elements in the composite were not needed for effective performance. Although Gage and Giaconia (1981) demonstrated a relationship between degree of implementation and degree of association with performance, what tended to remain unexplained was *why* particular combinations of teacher behavior led to gain and others did not, a question of theory. And this question leads to the most serious problems of process-product research.

A third, and most important reason for the erosion of the process-product program was its unabashedly empirical and nontheoretical tenor. Even as it moved to experimental treatments, the emphasis was pragmatically on what worked, rather than on why it worked. Causes were sought in behaviors, not in theoretically meaningful mechanisms or explanations. The perspective was that of engineering rather than that of science, or even of history. But, paraphrasing Aristotle, man (at least the non-Skinnerian among the scholarly species) is a theoretical animal. Humans seek to identify mechanisms or processes that will *explain why* stimuli elicit responses, why behaviors are associated with performances, and most compellingly, why some do under some circumstances and not under others. Even experiments that may help somewhat in distinguishing causes from co-occurrences do not necessarily explain. And the best scientific theory is not necessarily the one that predicts or controls best, but indeed that which renders the most comprehensive and compelling account consistent with the available evidence (Toulmin, 1961).

It is thus no surprise that the critics who found the process–product program wanting did so on theoretical grounds, not because it failed to yield significant correlations or F ratios. The problems associated with an absence of explanatory theory had been anticipated by Dunkin and Biddle (1974, e.g., pp. 428–430). Nearly a decade later, they were acknowledged by leaders in the process–product tradition, such as Good et al. (1983). Within the broad purview of process–product psychologists, critics typically sought to develop programs in which explanatory mediating variables were posited to intervene between teacher behavior and pupil performance, in the form of process → mediator → product. These mediators took several forms, which will be discussed thoroughly in the sections to follow.

The earliest was the Beginning Teacher Evaluation Study (BTES) search for the mechanism that would explain why direct instruction worked (Fisher et al., 1978). Their solution, guided by John Carroll's (1963) model of school learning, was *allocated time* and *task engagement*. They shifted the emphasis from the activities of teachers as causes to the activities of pupils as explanations, interpreting the latter as the intervening events that accounted for what direct instruction could accomplish that other forms of teaching (or nonteaching) did not. This research program will be discussed in the section that follows.

The student mediation program also sought for a mechanism

of explanation, and its proponents were not satisfied with time as a mediator. What were pupils doing with that time? How were they engaged? Engaged in what? These scholars drew from several neighboring fields to guide their work. Some took the information-processing perspectives of cognitive science and examined the ways in which pupils used time to reduce the complexity and make sense of the curriculum content presented. The active model of the learner as assimilator, as transformer, as apprehender of knowledge-as-presented (echoing Herbart's conception of the apperceptive mass) was applied to the classroom and the image began to develop of an active learner interacting with active teaching. What sense do pupils make of different forms of instruction? Rowe's (1974) work on wait-time took on renewed significance as the complex forms of information processing necessary for students to transform instruction were studied.

Other student mediation scholars sought their explanations not from cognitive psychology, but from social psychology and sociology, from the traditions of W. I. Thomas's "definition of the situation" as cloaked either in self-concept theory or, more recently, in Becker, Geer and Hughes's (1968) metaphor of the "performance–grade exchange." They directed the attention of the research community away from a focus on the classroom as a site for cognitive teaching and learning, as well as from traditional notions of pedagogy. Instead they looked at the classroom as a stage on which roles were played and the pupil's goals were to perform in ways that attracted good grades, high status, and minimum hassle. These perspectives from sociology served to connect the work on student mediation to research in the sociolinguistic and ethnographic traditions as well.

In their still-formidable work entitled *The Study of Teaching*, Dunkin and Biddle (1974) observed that while the process-product research had already been the most fruitful of the approaches reviewed (and this before the program's effort had really peaked), two aspects of that work were already perceptibly problematic. These were the continuing reliance on standardized achievement tests as the ultimate criterion of effectiveness and the overly molecular units of classroom analysis.

With respect to the measurement of achievement, they commented:

This is not only an insensitive variable, but it may be offmark for our purposes. Consider the finding that teacher use of higher cognitive demand leads to lower pupil achievement. It seems possible to us that lower cognitive demand is more efficient for putting across facts, while higher cognitive demand encourages independence of thought. The latter, of course, is not measured by standardized achievement tests. Hypotheses of this sort cannot be tested until more sensitive product criteria are developed and used in research on teaching. (p. 409)

Their views of the units of analysis were also critical:

It appears to us that any meaningful analysis of teaching must involve sequential elements. Indeed, perhaps *the greatest single flaw* [italics added] in much of the research we have reviewed is the persistent assumption that appears to underlie much of it — that teaching can somehow be reduced to a scalar value that can be indicated by a frequency of occurrence for some teaching behavior. We suspect, with Taba, that this simply is not true. Rather, effective teaching must consist of sequences of presentations that are planned carefully and conducted sensitively. Moreover, we find the sequential concepts we have reviewed to be insightful, exciting, suggestive. ... [But] even the clearest discussions of sequence are couched in murky, intuitive, analogistic phrases suggesting that investigators are still groping toward solutions to these complex problems. Thus, we can find relatively little evidence to back up our belief that the real breakthroughs in research on teaching should involve sequence. (ibid., p. 353)

Thus the volume that has served as the most powerful framer of the questions for the process–product research program via its comprehensive presage–context–process–product model found serious problems in the manner in which both processes and products are characterized. It may be recalled that Gage recognized similar limitations 10 years earlier. In spite of these misgivings, the process–product program has been conducted apace during the intervening years. Nevertheless, the possibility that the truncated, molecular conceptions of process fit uniquely well with the limited measures of product — thus inventing a classroom reality that "works" only within the confines of this research program — is an issue worth pondering.

As we shall see, many of the research programs that follow were stimulated by the desire to repair some flaw in the process–product paradigm, or to attend to phenomena ignored or invisible to its scholars. However, in contrast to the conception of paradigm shifts and scientific revolutions found in Kuhn, these more recent approaches rarely attend to everything treated in the process-product work *or* the missing aspect of teaching they have identified. Some of the newer approaches represent supplementary programs that examine particular aspects of teaching or learning in great detail while often themselves ignoring features of teaching highlighted in process-product work. Others, such as the classroom ethnographers, take a totally different perspective on teaching, but in so doing also lose sight of many aspects of the phenomenon of teaching highlighted in the older paradigm, As Merton (1975) led us to anticipate, the alternative research programs do not supplant one another so much as provide opportunities to examine particular aspects of teaching more closely. Each paradigm highlights a particular neighborhood on the synoptic map, leaving other territories dark and unexplored. No one has all the lines in the Great Conversation.

Time and Learning

Even as the process-product program was picking up speed in the early 1970s, a most significant variation on that program, dedicated to identifying the key mediators of teacher behavior in the activities of pupils, was initiated. The research staff of the Far West Regional Educational Laboratory was conducting the third phase of the Beginning Teacher Evaluation Study (BTES). Under the leadership of David Berliner, Charles Fisher, Leonard Cahen, and their colleagues, they were seeking an indicator of teacher effectiveness they could locate in the observable performance of pupils without waiting for end-of-year achievement tests. They were motivated to find such an indicator for two reasons. They wished to transfer the attention of the research-on-teaching community from concern for teacher behavior alone to more balanced consideration of the coordinate and immediate pupil responses to teaching. In addition, they felt that variations in some pupil indicator would provide a more sensitive estimate of the effects of teaching than the more distal product of achievement-test performance.

Consistent with our view that the field of research on teaching should be viewed as an ongoing dialogue or conversation among scholars, the starting point for their analysis was a critique of the adequacy of the logic of the process-product program. Note that their critique did not rest on a failure of the program's empirical findings nor on an empirical anomaly. In Berliner's (1979) words:

> The investigators [in BTES] became increasingly dissatisfied with the process-product approach since it appeared that certain illogical elements were inherent in the design of a process-product study of classroom teaching. For example, how could the number or percentage of teacher verbal communications coded as praise statements in November influence results on achievement test items given in May? ... How could anyone expect to discover a relationship between a variable such as time spent lecturing on ecology and achievement test items that measure dictionary usage? The latter occurs when investigators use instruments that code teacher behavior of various sorts and correlate that behavior with broad-spectrum tests of reading achievement.
>
> At first it appeared that correlational approaches using the process-product research paradigm were inherently deficient. Some of our colleagues argued that only by recourse to true experiments could the situation be remedied. But true experimental designs used in the investigation of teaching and learning in classrooms also have certain flaws. The most serious of these are that such designs do not reflect the complexities of the classroom, with its myriad interactions; they do not reflect the dynamic quality of the classroom, with its ever-changing events; nor can they, typically, develop an appropriate time perspective since the acquisition of knowledge in the classroom is best conceived of as a multiyear process. Thus, experimental designs that reflect the process-product framework often suffer from problems of ecological validity.
>
> If correlational studies were to be conducted in natural classroom environments, which would appear to give them more potential external validity, then the logical and hypothetical causal flow of events in the process-product model needed to be modified. Researchers on the Beginning Teacher Evaluation Study proposed a simple modification of the process-product approach to the study of classroom learning. The modification is based on the belief that what a teacher does at any one moment while working in a circumscribed content area affects a student primarily at only that particular moment and in that particular content area. The link between teacher behavior and student achievement is, therefore, the ongoing student behavior in the classroom learning situation. The logic continues in this way. What a teacher does to foster learning in a particular content area becomes important only if a student is engaged with *appropriate* curriculum content. Appropriate curriculum content is defined as content that is logically related to the criterion and is at an easy level of difficulty for a particular student. ... The vari-

able used in BTES research is the accrued engaged time in a particular content area using materials that are not difficult for the student. This complex variable is called Academic Learning Time (ALT). . . .

In this conception of research on teaching, the content area the student is working on must be specified precisely, the task engagement of the student must be judged, the level of the difficulty of the task must be rated, and time must be measured. The constructed variable of ALT, then, stands between measures of teaching and measures of student achievement. (pp. 122-125)

Berliner locates the BTES research on Academic Learning Time at the intersection of three research programs: the process-product tradition of research on teaching; the work of Carroll (1963), of Bloom (1968; 1976), and of Harnischfeger and Wiley (1976), all deriving from Carroll's model of school learning; and the literature of instructional design, especially programed instruction, with its concern for the control of error rates.

The decision to take the conception of error control from the field of instructional design led to the most significant weakness in the program. It is certainly true that error control is important in skill acquisition. Low error rates are particularly important because of the nature of standardized achievement tests as criteria. The observation that high error rates are associated with poor performance can be nearly tautological. The tasks of classroom life are themselves a sample of the same universe of questions from which are drawn the items of the standardized tests. In that sense, classroom discourse is a series of achievement tests in dialogue or in seatwork. (In fact, numerous studies have demonstrated that most teaching involves very little explicit instruction by the teacher. Instead, assignments are distributed and subsequent student work is monitored.) The youngster with high error rates is not simply learning less because of his errors. His errors are a signal that he is learning less. Moreover, the estimation of task difficulty has become one of the most troublesome in the ALT research program, and has generally been given far less attention in both the research and policy literatures than has the conception of academically engaged time.

In this work as well, the extent to which the significance of relationships is ultimately tethered to performance on standardized achievement tests remains troubling. At least two recent studies, by Armbruster, Stevens, and Rosenshine (1977) at the Center for the Study of Reading, and by Freeman et al. (1983) at the Institute for Research on Teaching, have demonstrated the extent of the mismatch between what is taught in schools and what is measured on standardized tests. Doyle (1983) summarized the results of the study by Armbruster et al. thus:

> They found that the overlap between the texts and the standardized tests was low. The reading curricula tended to emphasize "comprehension skills that appear to require inference, interpretation, identification of relationships, and synthesis." ... The tests, on the other hand, tended to focus on "factual items entailing locating information in the presented text." (p. 181)

Given the demonstrated mismatch between the texts of instruction and the tests of achievement, will curricular relevance within the ALT program be defined by correspondence with instructional goals and materials, or by correlation with test-measured long-term outcomes? The answer is significant, not only for the ALT program, but for all other programs that employ outcome measures in their work.

Most important in the theoretical aspect of this work is the influence of Carroll's model of school learning and its choice of *time* as the central construct for the teaching–learning transaction. Carroll's model posits five variables which, in their direct effects and interactions, account for the amount learned on particular school tasks. Three of these constructs describe attributes of the learner — ability, aptitude, and perseverance. Two constructs describe attributes of the instruction — opportunity to learn and quality of instruction. Most important, the values of three of the variables can be expressed as units of time. Thus, *aptitude* is defined as the amount of time needed by a learner to achieve mastery of a particular school task. *Opportunity* to learn is defined as the amount of time provided by the teacher for the learning of a particular task by a particular student. *Perseverance*, the student analogue of opportunity, is the amount of time a learner devotes to the job of mastering the task in question.

The other two constructs, ability and quality of instruction, are defined in more qualitative terms. *Ability* describes the individual's mode or style of learning relative to the task at hand. *Quality of instruction*, so central to any research on teaching, remains frustratingly elusive. It represents the extent to which the instruction provided adequately matches the character of the student's ability. Berliner's treatment of task difficulty appears to be an indirect way of representing this important concept of instructional quality. Certainly the discussion of curriculum-appropriate tasks is also relevant to this notion. But the continuing difficulty among both process–product investigators and the ALT proponents in dealing adequately with the issues of substantive instructional quality remains a nagging weakness in these research programs. In fact, as we shall see in the course of this chapter, it is the common flaw in all the extant programs of research on teaching.

Though it was initiated by a critique of the process–product program, we can see that the ALT program itself continues to employ many of its predecessor's characteristic tactics and distinctions. It is concerned with the relationships among *variables*, it focuses on individual students (rather than the collectivity of the classroom) as units of analysis, its conception of student learning remains a rather passive one (compared to the active processing view of contemporary cognitive psychology or the ethnography of communication), and it continues the disaggregation of the events of classroom life. That is, despite Berliner's eloquent attack on the process–product paradigm's inability to capture the "complexities of the classroom, with its myriad interactions" and "the dynamic quality of the classroom, with its ever-changing events," the ALT program as well falls short of that richness. ALT remains a more explanation-oriented, mediational variant of process–product research. It certainly has forsaken its parent's home in some significant ways, but it remains an unmistakable member of the extended family. Gage (1978) had criticized the ALT emphasis on engaged time with the observation that time is an empty vessel. Unless a better account could be rendered of how that time was being used by students, the addition of another layer of variables could hardly make the claim of theoretical progress. But the BTES's identification of the need to fill the gap between teaching and academic achievement with a representation of how and what students were processing served to formulate the next critical task for the field of research on teaching — a task most directly addressed by those who labor in the research program we call the student mediation of instruction, to which we now turn.

Pupil Cognition and the Mediation of Teaching

The Academic Learning Time research program shifted the emphasis of researchers away from the study of relationships between the actions of the teacher and the distant outcomes of pupil achievement. Its scholars brought attention to the inferred thought processes of the pupils themselves. Yet, consistent with the traditions of psychological behaviorism, the ALT program relied wholly on observed teacher and student behavior, and on the characteristics of task performance, as the bases for these inferences.

In the student mediation programs, reviewed by Wittrock in this volume, we encounter for the first time the influence of several new perspectives on the study of teaching. From within psychology, the effect of the cognitive revolution can be observed, in particular studies of social cognition. We also can detect influences from the psychology of personality and the study of self-concept. From other disciplines, we observe the influence of sociology, both in theoretical formulation and in choice of methods. We shall see that this research program comprises the potential bridge between the traditional quantitative psychological perspectives of the process–product and ALT approaches and the predominantly qualitative strategies of classroom ecology research, with its strong links to sociolinguistics and ethnography.

The overriding questions for those who pursue the student mediation program are "How do students make sense of the instruction they encounter in the classroom? What are the immediate and intermediate-term processes engendered in students by teaching?" It should be recalled that the concept of mediation arose out of the stimulus–response (S–R) paradigm in psychology as learning theorists like Tolman and Osgood attempted to understand what processes mediated between the *S* and the *R*. Similarly, the fundamental process of teaching is assumed in process–product research to be a link between teacher behavior and eventual student performance. When you attend to the possibility that the action is not direct, that it is not im-mediate, not unmediated, you then posit an intervening process through which the initial cause is transformed into its eventually observed effect. For the time-on-task researcher, Academic Learning Time serves as the proxy for such an intervening process. For those who seek to fill the "empty vessel" of time with more descriptive accounts of what is happening in the minds of learners between the input of instruction and the output of achievement (hence, the *mediating* processes that occupy that middle ground), a fuller account is needed. A proxy will not do. A direct account of the mediating mechanisms is the goal of research.

In the pupil mediation literature, two sources for these accounts can be identified. Mehan (1979) has observed that the complexity of classroom life for students is twofold. "Participation in classroom lessons involves the integration of academic knowledge and social or interactional knowledge" (p. 34). These two kinds of accomplishment are the topics of research on the social mediation and the intellectual mediation of classroom life, respectively. The first, and thus far the more popular, emerges from the sociological traditions in which classroom work is seen as an exchange of performance for grades (Becker et al., 1968) or some equivalent underlying process not immediately obvious to the observer who views classroom settings as occasions for teaching and learning. This approach to analysis emerges, at least in part, from the distinction between manifest and latent functions, or between anticipated and unanticipated consequences, both distinctions presented by Merton to explain some of the complexities of social processes. In these analyses, the sociologist is asked to peer beneath the apparent surface meanings and purposes of participants in a social setting to discern the underlying processes, goals, and perspectives. This tradition has been the source for the important efforts regarding the "hidden curriculum" of the school and classroom, wherein what is hidden are precisely those latent features not explicitly treated in the apparent curriculum.

One example of such work is a study by L. Anderson (1984). She examines the ways in which primary-grade children cope with seatwork, that ubiquitous element in the life of schoolchildren. Whereas the process–product researcher would have correlated frequency of seatwork (or proportion of classroom time spent in seatwork) with student achievement, and the Academic Learning Time scholar would have observed the proportion of seatwork time during which the student was apparently engaged along with the degree of difficulty of the tasks with which the student was working, Anderson proceeds to record student comments to themselves and to classmates during assignments and to interview the students about their assignments after observing them at work. Her focus is on what the students are thinking and feeling as they work on their tasks, on what these phenomena reveal about the mediation of instruction by the students.

"There! I didn't understand that, but I got it done," offers one 6-year-old. "I'm almost done — just two more," or "How far are you?" are typical of the most frequently overheard student exchanges, rather than "What answer did you get?" In general, Anderson remarks on the frequency with which the essential goal of the students is to complete an assignment rather than to comprehend a task. They are exchanging performance for evaluation and approval.

She also detects differences between low and high achievers in the strategies employed to complete the work. Low-achieving students are observed to employ any strategy available to complete an assignment whether or not the completed page makes sense. They do not appear to have developed the metacognitive strategies needed to identify whether their work is correct. Confusion is such a constant companion during seatwork that they appear to assume that confusion is supposed to accompany all academic work. They rarely seek help to allay the difficulty. In contrast, when high-achieving students get confused, they treat that state as problematic and seek help immediately.

Anderson's study exemplifies both the strengths and weaknesses of work on student mediation. Characterization of student thought processes and motivations surrounding school tasks is accomplished with a sensitivity unavailable in other research programs. But trade-offs are necessary. The tasks themselves are not carefully described. We get too little sense of how variations among tasks, or among forms of teaching, relate to differences in how students mediate those instructional presentations. As with the paradigms discussed earlier, far too little attention is devoted to differences in the content of subject matter being taught. In focusing down on the description of how students respond to teaching, the scholar in this approach provides quite incomplete portrayals of other aspects of the teaching situation. We thus learn important new things about teaching from this research, but also forgo parts of the portrayal available from the work in other research programs.

The second stream of work on the pupil mediation of instruction has developed from the current applications of cognitive psychology to the learning of school subjects. This work has been grounded in the recognition that in even the most simple of cognitive tasks, learning is not a passive process in which the learner incorporates veridical representations of what has been taught. Indeed, the essence of any act of learning or problem solving is the active role played by the learner in transforming the ostensible message (the nominal stimulus in the language of S–R psychology) of instruction into the learner's own cognitive structures. Whether discussed in the language of nominal and functional stimuli, or of the Piagetian's balance between assimilation and accommodation, or of Ausubel's advance organizers and subsumptions, or the information-processing psychologist's task environment and its transformation into a problem space, or of Herbart's appreciative mass, the central message is always the same. The learner does not respond to the instruction per se. The learner responds to the instruction as transformed, as actively apprehended. Thus, to understand why learners respond (or fail to respond) as they do, ask not what they were taught, but what sense they rendered of what they were taught. The consequences of teaching can only be understood as a function of what that teaching stimulates the learner to do with material.

We can thus envision two parallel streams of action traversing between teacher and learner. Teaching is mediated by the sense the learner makes of the social context of the classroom situation — the way turns are distributed, the character of praise and blame, the implicit standards of performance, the cues employed to signal opportunities to participate, or changes of task and the like. Parallel to the learner's active interpretation of the social reality of the classroom, there exists a mental representation and construction of the cognitive content of what is being taught. New concepts are constantly compared to and assimilated within older ones; metacognitive strategies are deployed, accurately or not, to direct and monitor intellectual skills and specific pieces of knowledge needed for understanding a new principle or perspective. The schematic figure below, abstracted from the larger synoptic model presented earlier, represents the simultaneity of the two processes in the learner. Unquestionably, both processes are occurring concurrently in the minds of students. Ironically, the research community has seemed capable of thinking about only one of these at a time. With the signal exception of the empirical and theoretical work of Walter Doyle (1983), the two streams of mediational processes — social and intellectual — have been pursued by quite separate communities of investigators.

TEACHING→SOCIAL MEDIATION→COGNITIVE MEDIATION→ LEARNING

To understand the parallel between the social mediation and the cognitive information-processing perspectives, it is useful to compare key statements of theoretical propositions from central figures in each domain: Clifford Geertz (1973), the social anthropologist, and Herbert Simon (1957), the information-processing psychologist. Geertz (1973) asserts:

The concept of culture I espouse ... is essentially a semiotic one. Believing with Max Weber that man is an animal suspended in webs of significance he himself has spun, I take culture to be those webs, and the analysis of it to be therefore not an experimental science in search of law but an interpretive one in search of meaning. It is explication I am after, construing social expressions on their surface enigmatical. (p. 5)

In a similar vein, Simon (1957) defines the concept of bounded rationality:

The capacity of the human mind for formulating and solving complex problems is very small compared with the size of the problem whose solution is required for objectively rational behavior in the real world — or even a reasonable approximation to such objective reality. ... the first consequence of the principle of bounded rationality is that the intended rationality of an actor requires him to construct a simplified model of the real situation in order to deal with it. He behaves rationally with respect to this model, and such behavior is not even approximately optimal with respect to the real world. To predict his behavior, we must understand the way in which this simplified model is constructed, and its construction will certainly be related to his psychological properties as a perceiving, thinking, and learning animal. (pp. 198-199)

The two conceptions are remarkably parallel, each arguing that the construction of reality, whether sociocultural reality in the form of webs of significance or cognitive reality in the form of problem spaces, is the central process explaining human behavior and choice. To understand why individuals behave as they do, one must understand both the grounds on which they render their simplifications or constructions, and the particular constructions they create. The difference between the psychologist's account and the sociologist's is the grounds. For the psychologist they have to do with the species-general cognitive limitations and predispositions of the individual information processor, as well as with the intellectual history of that individual that shows up as schemata, scripts, preconceptions, prototypes, metacognitive strategies, expectations, attributions, subjective probabilities, and the like. For the sociologist, they are properties associated with the groups of which the individual is a member — SES, ethnicity, occupation, religion, and the like. They may also be called expectations, attributions, or roles (concepts which, like the cognitive psychologist's scripts, are simply parallel metaphors from the theater), but the theoretical explanation for their sources is different. In that sense, the sociologist and the anthropologist will often look alike, although the latter will work harder to see the world from the perspective of the phenomenological categories that function to parse the world of the subjects themselves.

For the microethnographer, or constitutive ethnographer, whose work will be discussed in the next section of the chapter, the most important reality may be that of the group or setting within which the individual and his colleagues function. They will have established rules by which the group members interact, rules that define the legitimate and illegitimate, allowable and forbidden activities of group members. These certainly function within limits set by the larger cultural and social groups of which members are a part, but the smaller school or classroom groups define further rules of the game.

For both the cognitive psychologist and the social anthropologist, therefore, the task of explaining the life of classrooms, the fate of instructional activities, and the social interactions that accompany them, is a matter of discovering the simplification and reconstruction of reality employed by the participants to transform the world as presented into a world with which they can work. The question is not what teaching is most effective, but what meaning is given to the teaching (or is given by teacher and students to the events of classroom life) and what are the grounds for those constructions.

Most of the social psychological work on student mediation

of instruction has not followed the format of the Anderson research cited earlier. Instead, investigators (e.g., Weinstein, 1983) have attempted to understand the more stable ways in which students regularly interpret teacher comments and actions. Those student mediations are treated almost like enduring states, like traits, perceptions, attributions, or evaluations employed to make sense of one's own behavior as well as that of others. The studies rarely trace such mediations through to the outcomes of particular instructional episodes. Instead, the ostensible mediators are treated as ends in themselves.

In contrast, those engaged in the study of cognitive mediators of instruction (e.g., Peterson & Swing, 1982; Winne & Marx, 1982) generally use interviews or stimulated recall to collect reports of student thought processes during and immediately after instruction. They may also conduct experiments in which students are taught to use the hypothesized mediators and the effects of such use on achievement are monitored. In most such cases, the mediators studied are generic, at the level of strategies, attentional focus, broad schemata, and the like. They rarely get to the subject-specific level of student thought processes studied by cognitive psychologists of learning. Important findings from all this work indicate the unreliability of judgments regarding student attention made by outside observers. Students who look as if they are attending may not be mediating the instruction productively.

As indicated earlier, the work of Doyle stands out as an exception to the observation that cognitive and social mediation are never studied together. In his essay on academic work (Doyle, 1983), he presents an analysis of the relationships between the cognitive difficulties presented by a task and the challenges of accomplishing such tasks in the social and evaluative environment of classrooms. His work serves not only as a conceptual bridge between these two islands in the student mediation research program, but as a provocative link to the research on classroom ecology, a research program deriving mainly from disciplines outside of psychology, to be discussed in the next section.

Classroom Ecology

The approaches to the study of classroom teaching we have reviewed thus far share a fundamental family membership in the process-product tradition. All except the social perception stream of the mediational program derive from psychology. But as we enter the world of research on classroom ecology, we encounter an utterly different set of intellectual traditions. Not only are these more often qualitative than quantitative methodologically, but their parent disciplines are more frequently anthropology, sociology, and linguistics. The emphasis of process-product research on the essential role of achievement outcomes, on the relative decontextualization of analyses, on the objectification of data in the search for positive laws, is typically missing in this family of research. Missing also, however, are the propositions that can be readily translated into principles for policy or maxims for practice. For those concerned with the value of research for guiding practice through the aggregation and accumulation of usable knowledge, the yield of research in this program is questionable. For those committed to a view of social science as a source of criticism and new questions rather than practical answers, the yield is considerable.

This is an extended family of inquiries, not a simple, tightly knit one. The family includes ethnographers like Erickson (1973), Heath (1983), Wolcott (1973) or Phillips (1983); sociologists like Delamont (e.g., Delamont & Atkinson, 1980), or Lightfoot (1983); psychologists like Jackson (1968) or Smith (Smith & Geoffrey, 1968); sociolinguists like Cadzen (this volume), Mehan (1979), or Green (1983); curriculum and teaching specialists like Doyle (1977). Even these classifications are difficult to make because the work so readily crosses disciplinary boundaries in the social sciences and even the humanities.

Studies within this research program range from the microanalysis of interactions, both verbal and nonverbal, within a single reading group lesson (McDermott, 1976) or over several sessions of a morning "show and tell" in a kindergarten/first grade, using videotape to preserve the smallest units of interactional detail (Florio, 1978), to the macroanalysis of an entire high school with data gathered over a two-week period (Lightfoot, 1983) or of a full community in relation to its high school, with data gathered over an entire year (Peshkin, 1978).

It is important to appreciate the differences between the kinds of questions posed and propositions offered by scholars in this general tradition and those whose work we have considered thus far. The most articulate spokesperson for this research program is the distinguished anthropologist Clifford Geertz, whose work I have briefly cited earlier. I shall quote from two of his writings: "Thick Description" (Geertz, 1973) and "Blurred Genres" (1983), in which he strives to contrast these two traditions of investigation, the positive and the interpretive, as well as to explain to those of us who have been raised in the positivist milieu what constitutes the interpretive research program. In a statement quoted earlier in the chapter, Geertz (1973) observes:

> The concept of culture I espouse ... is essentially a semiotic one. Believing with Max Weber that man is an animal suspended in webs of significance he himself has spun, I take culture to be those webs, and the analysis of it to be therefore not an experimental science in search of law but an interpretive one in search of meaning. It is explication I am after, construing social expressions on their surface enigmatical. (p. 5)

Geertz thus sees the purpose of his investigations to be "an interpretive one in search of meaning" rather than "an experimental science in search of law." A number of years later, he wrote an essay in which he observed that the boundaries between traditional scholarly genres had become blurred, and not only within the anthropological field. Geertz (1983) asserts that "many social scientists have turned away from a laws and instances ideal of explanation toward a cases and interpretations one.... Analogies drawn from the humanities are coming to play the kind of role in sociological understanding that analogies drawn from the crafts and technology have long played in physical understanding" (p. 19). Geertz (1983) characterizes the vocation of social scientists as "trying to discover order in collective life":

> Interpretive explanation ... trains its attention on what institutions, actions, images, utterances, events, customs, all the usual objects of social scientific interest, mean to those whose institutions, actions, customs, and so on they are. As a result, it issues not in laws like Boyle's, or forces like Volta's, or mechanisms like Darwin's, but in constructions like Burkhardt's, Weber's or Freud's: systematic unpackings of the conceptual world....
> The manner of these constructions itself varies: Burckhardt portrays, Weber models, Freud diagnoses. But they all represent attempts to formulate how this people or that ... makes sense to itself

and, understanding that, what we understand about social order, historical change, or psychic functioning in general. Inquiry is directed at cases or sets of cases, and toward the particular features that mark them off; but its aims are as far-reaching as those of mechanics or physiology: to distinguish the materials of human experience.

... In the social sciences, or at least in those that have abandoned a reductionist conception of what they are about, the analogies are coming more and more from the contrivances of cultural performance than from those of physical manipulation — from theater, painting, grammar, literature, law, play. What the lever did for physics, the chess move promises to do for sociology. (p. 21)

In the research programs we have been discussing thus far, certain shared assumptions have been apparent in spite of the contrasts drawn among them. The teacher has been very much the center of classroom life, the source or starting point for teaching. Whether the teacher's verbal or physical behavior has been seen as the immediate cause of learning, as in the process-product tradition, or as the agent whose messages are mediated, as in the ALT or student mediation programs, that it is the starting point for analysis has not been a matter for controversy. In the research programs that collectively define the study of classroom ecology, however, this matter of causal direction is itself problematic.

Green's (1983) review of the linguistic perspective in research on teaching captures some of the central assumptions of this program:

Central to this conceptualization is the view of classrooms as communicative environments in which the events that make up everyday life are constructed as part of the interactions between teachers and students.... From this perspective, events evolve during interactions as teachers and students work together to meet instructional goals. Therefore, classroom events ... are dynamic activities constructed by teachers and students as they process, build on, and work with both their own and others' messages and behaviors....

The goal of this work is to understand the nature of teaching-learning processes from the perspective of the participants and to identify those factors that support learning and communicative performance that may lead to evaluation of student ability. (pp. 355, 357)

In an article in the same volume, Hamilton (1983) argues that there are four criteria for ecological research, criteria that bear strong similarity to those enunciated by Green. These characteristics are (a) attention to the interaction between persons and their environments, especially in reciprocal terms rather than in terms of simple directional causality from teachers to students; (b) treating teaching and learning as continuously interactive processes rather than isolating a few factors in the system and labeling them as "cause" and "effect"; (c) seeing the classroom context as nested within other contexts — the school, the community, the family, the culture — all of which influence what can be observed in the classroom itself; and (d) treating unobservable processes, such as thoughts, attitudes, feelings, or perceptions of the participants, as important sources of data.

A number of chapters in this volume treat the growing body of work that participates in this research program. These include the chapters by Erickson, Cazden, and Evertson and Green. I run the risk of lumping together what many participating investigators view as distinct research enterprises. Surely the disciplinary traditions from which participants derive are diverse. They range from anthropology and sociolinguistics to sociology and ecological psychology. They include in their number both ethnomethodologists and symbolic interactionists. Yet, when contrasted with the psychologists, whether behaviorist or mentalist, whose work has dominated the programs reviewed earlier (and the study of teacher cognition to be discussed in the next section), they constitute a distinctive family of inquiry.

Most of these research programs derive from disciplinary roots much older, and certainly independent of, the mainstream research-on-teaching traditions represented by process-product programs. Nevertheless, within the recent history of research on teaching, they have jointly played a critical role in the great conversation, a role in which they raise questions about the findings and assumptions of the dominant tradition. They are especially interested in circumstances wherein the generalizations of process-product studies may fail to hold for social or cultural minorities, or under particular circumstances, both concerns deriving from the strong anthropological and sociological perspectives of these researchers. When process-product researchers summarize the results of their studies in general prescriptive terms such as "increase engaged time" or "increase wait-times" or "begin the school year with clearly formulated rules," the classroom ecology researchers ask how teachers might concretely and locally accomplish such ends. Here again, they are also wont to ask under what cultural conditions these general prescriptions will be found incomplete or even dead wrong.

Researchers in this program have somewhat different perspectives on the concept of "effectiveness" as well. Process-product researchers focus predominantly on criteria of effectiveness lying outside the immediate classroom setting being observed, that is, achievement measured by end-of-year standardized achievement tests or end-of-unit norm-referenced performance tests. Classroom ecology researchers tend to look for criteria of effectiveness within the situation. These include equality of opportunities to participate (rather than participation frequencies as a function of social class, ethnicity, or prior academic standing); indicators of clear communications of meaning between teacher and students (especially focal in multiethnic classrooms where teacher and students may be from different cultural backgrounds); or smoothness of interchanges, transitions, or other commonplace classroom events.

In addition, they are particularly sensitive to what students do in order to convey the *appearance* of understanding or correct performance. They are concerned about poor students being so judged because they have not learned to "look smart" or "talk smart." The complex interplay between the hidden and manifest curriculum is apparent in these analyses of how learning the presentation of self as a good student relates to being treated as one. That treatment, in turn, can lead to subsequent opportunities to learn (e.g., placement in a higher reading group, more frequent opportunities to respond) that ultimately produce higher achievement and more positive self-esteem.

The most frequent misunderstanding of this research program occurs when it is characterized as "qualitative" and the other programs are deemed "quantitative." This view assumes that the different research programs are essentially looking at the same phenomena for similar purposes, but that process-product or positivistic scholars use larger samples and carefully prepared observation schedules subsequently to be analyzed quantitatively. Interpretive or sociolinguistic or ethnographic researchers employ lined yellow pads, write down everything they see for extended durations of time in very few (frequently only one) classrooms with the intention of summarizing their findings in narrative form. The contrast is erroneously drawn between quantitative science and qualitative story-telling.

As can be learned in the several chapters on this topic found in the present volume (Erickson; Cazden; Evertson & Green) the most important differences between the research programs are substantive rather than methodological. While it may well be true that interpretive classroom process researchers are likely to eschew observation scales for open-ended observations, the important differences lie in the conceptions of learning, classrooms, and teaching held by the investigators, as well as the implicit perspectives on the goals of educational research and the interests served by such activity.

While process–product researchers view classrooms as reducible to discrete events and behaviors which can be noted, counted, and aggregated for purposes of generalization across settings and individuals, interpretive scholars view classrooms as socially and culturally organized environments. Individual participants in those environments contribute to the organization and to the definition of meanings. They are actively engaged in "making sense" in the setting, taking both senses of that phrase. They both discern the meanings intended by other actors and they engage in the continuing invention and reformulation of new meanings.

Those personal meanings become the focal point for inquiry, in contrast to the behaviors that focus the effort of the process-product scholars. Here we see the work of the student mediation program intersecting with that of the classroom process, interpretive, sociolinguistic scholars. This program is concerned with the significance of events to the actors themselves, both those shared by all participants in a context and those that are interpreted differently by individuals in the setting who come from very different social, linguistic, and/or cultural backgrounds.

This program is thus comparative in at least two ways. Every context is seen as embedded or nested within other contexts. Life in classrooms is understood as a function, not only of the jointly produced local meanings of the particular classroom group, but also as influenced by the larger contexts in which the class is embedded — the school, the community, the society, the culture. Moreover, since children of different backgrounds move in and out of the classroom from contrasting social and language communities, they will be making sense of classroom life employing different frames of reference.

Reflecting the influence of anthropology and linguistics, this program is also comparative in a second sense. Studies are often conducted in settings that are culturally different from the typical American school, and contrasts are drawn with schools and classrooms in other cultures. This frequently reflects not only the value of contextual contrasts in clarifying the interpretation of a phenomenon under study, but the tendency of scholars in this program to be particularly concerned with the special problems encountered in the educational systems by pupils (and even teachers) who are relatively powerless.

Research is thus often conducted for the purpose of showing how "the system" fails to serve the children of the poor, the linguistically or culturally different, ethnic minorities, and other disadvantaged populations. Through meticulous examination of the most commonplace events of classroom life — turn allocations, modes of explanation, nonverbal messages of praise and blame, and the like — classroom ecology researchers show how a hidden curriculum to which the less advantaged are not privy can control access to success with the manifest curriculum. In this way, much research in this tradition takes on a more radical or critical political tone relative to the process-product approaches.

The study of particular instances of classroom failure — the Anglo teacher who misunderstands and is misunderstood by Hispanic youngsters; the native Hawaiian reading group that fails because the participation structure violates principles of discourse learned in the home; the native American reservation classrooms in which achievement does not rise until native American teachers are brought in to teach; the South Boston kindergarten/first grade where the Italian-American child cannot figure out how to get a turn — often are the focal points of the cases carefully described by classroom process researchers. The implicit logic of the inquiries is that analysis of occasions where the typical flow of instruction breaks down or falters presents a strategic site for research. Much like the approach of neuroanatomists, who study the effects of brain lesions in order better to understand the normal workings of the brain, or of personality psychologists who investigate deviant behavior as a way of discovering general principles, the classroom ethnographer studies concrete, particular cases where what is typical or expected is likely to be violated. But he has interest not only in characterizing that particular setting, but in discovering universals as well.

In this regard, the classroom ethnographer frequently has his or her own perspective on teacher effectiveness, and will even accede to using the standardized test score as criterion. Instead of locating effectiveness in the specific behaviors of the teacher, the classroom process researcher looks for the "independent variable" in the reflexive participation structures produced jointly by the teacher and students. Although the effectiveness criterion is the same one employed by the process-product researchers, the essential conception of process is different.

Erickson (Volume 2) makes a strong argument that the logic of inquiry for the interpretive researcher is from the concrete particular to the universal. Where this differs from the inductive positivist is that the interpretive researcher does not sample instances or elements across a wide range of concrete particulars as the basis for inferring universals. Instead, he studies a concrete particular case in detail, aiming to develop as full a model as possible of the situation and the contexts in which it is nested. From anhalysis of concrete cases and examination of commonalities across detailed particularizations of them, generalizations are sought and tested. This approach contrasts with the characterization of positivist researchers who employ partial specifications of a setting that are sampled far more widely across instanes of the same sort of setting.

It is thus the ecosystem of learner, classroom, teacher, school, and community that serves as the theoretical ideal unit of inquiry for the interpretive researcher. It is not the behavior or thought of the individual teacher or student. The participants are seen as jointly constructing the meanings in those situations, and those meanings are subject to continuous renegotiation and revision. Individual behavior, interpretations, meanings, or motives can be understood only in the context of the more general system of organized relations.

How well do interpretive researchers achieve the ideal they seek? What problems do they encounter as they attempt to understand the complexities of classroom life? Although our discussion of research in the classroom ecology program is not yet complete, it is perhaps judicious to examine it critically at this point. The ambition of the classroom ecology program has not always been matched by its accomplishments. It is, unfortunately, far easier to speak of the importance of capturing reflexively constructed social realities, or of documenting the consequences of nested contexts, than it is to conduct the research. The challenges of producing a fully specified model of a classroom situation, of eschewing generalization for particularization, or of portraying the world from the perspectives of the participants rather than that of researchers, are formidable. It is especially difficult to pursue interpretive studies with appropriate levels of reliability and precision. Those who pursue research in the classroom ecology program are prone to no fewer problems of both substance and method than are their colleagues who conduct research in the other paradigms we have reviewed.

A major problem is the tendency toward ambivalence with respect to generalization from case to case and from a particular case to the world at large. Although Geertz speaks wisely of generalizing within rather than across cases in ethnographies, too frequently we find educational researchers making sweeping general statements based on woefully limited data. Inferences that demand careful cross-site analyses, for example, are based on examination of a single case, or on several cases whose variations do not reflect principles of theoretical sampling.

Despite the criticisms that process-product researchers are guilty of looking at the complexities of classroom life only superficially, a few variables at a time, many classroom ethnographers limit themselves to examining particular features of classrooms in meticulous detail (e.g., participation patterns, uses of language), while themselves ignoring other central aspects of teaching, subject matter, or instructional tasks entirely. Contexts outside the classroom are too often described in the most general terms, subsequently to be ignored, or given short shrift, in the explanations of classroom interaction that follow. This occurs in spite of rhetoric regarding the importance of understanding the multiplicity of layered environments within which individuals and groups function. Research methods are often documented poorly or incompletely, leaving the reader to guess how certain data were collected or how frequently particular observations or interviews were conducted. The logic of inferences from data to conclusions is not always specified, thus leaving the reader either to trust in the integrity and wisdom of the researcher or to reject the claims entirely. These are a few of the problems that can beset research in the classroom ecology program.

Since this perspective is somewhat alien to the majority of researchers on teaching who have, like the author, been raised as psychologists (or at least with the unquestioned assumptions of positivist and reductionist social science), it may be helpful to think of an analogy from biology. It is certainly possible to argue that the natural starting point for biological inquiry and discourse is the individual cell, for it is the building block of all other forms of life or biological structures. Biology is therefore the study of cells, their characteristics and functions, and the ways cells aggregate to form organs, organ systems, and organisms.

Alternatively, it can be asserted that the organism, that entity capable of independent existence and functioning, is the appropriate unit of analysis. Starting from the organism, one would then ask how individual organs function to enable the organism's activities and how equilibrium among the various components of the organism's total structure is maintained. One would thus ask how the parts of the organism are organized into the functioning whole which is the organism itself.

Finally (though by no means exhaustively), one could posit that neither cells nor organisms are adequate as units of inquiry, for each is no more than a part of the natural whole, which is the community or ecosystem. It is as impossible to understand the workings of any individual organism independent of its ecosystem as it is impossible to define the functions of a cell independent of the organized system of organs and organ systems to which it contributes.

This example is presented simply to illustrate a biological analogue to the units-of-inquiry problem encountered in the study of teaching and learning in classrooms. Whether the individual teaching behavior, the coordinated activity of a teacher (or a learner) over an extended period of time, or the ecosystem of a total classroom — teacher and pupils viewed as reflexively causing one another's behavior — is the proper starting point for inquiry is, in principle, not answerable. Each starting point is a legitimate consequence of contrasting disciplinary and methodological assumptions. Each carries consequences for the questions that can be asked and the issues that can be entertained.

For the present discussion, this starting point has been selected quite differently in the process–product and the interpretive/ethnographic research programs.

We can therefore see how the various characteristics of the interpretive/qualitative/ethnographic/sociolinguistic research program of the classroom ecology genre are linked together. Definition of the unit of inquiry, emphasis on the personal perspectives of the participants, focus on concrete and particular, identification with the powerless, a particular view of verification and generalization, and a comparative orientation are all features of these approaches. Surely there are sharp battles among members of this broad research program, who often see the differences separating them as serious and profound. But compared to the assumptions and methods shared by most of the research programs discussed earlier, the differences are relatively small.

CLASSROOM PROCESS AND COGNITIVE SCIENCE RESEARCH

There is a striking similarity between some aspects of research in the traditions of school ethnography and of cognitive science. Both approaches ascribe substantial cognitive and/or social organization to the participants in their studies, and assume that prior knowledge, experience, or attitude frames the new encounters and their interpretation. Moreover, both approaches assume that the performances being viewed are rule governed. One of the central goals of research in both traditions is to analyze the observed behavior in meticulous detail in order to infer an underlying set of rules which would explain the observed variations. The system of rules for the cognitive scientist is often expressed in the form of a computer simulation program, or if memory organization and processes are in focus, as a semantic network or flow diagram. The system of rules for the ethnographer is typically presented in narrative form, or as a set of propositions.

It is likely that the similarity is due to a common source for research in both traditions. Both cognitive science and sociolinguists (which underlies much of what we currently call classroom microethnography) were born in the middle 1960s under the influence of Chomsky's (1957) transformational grammar. Miller, Galanter, and Pribram's (1960) *Plans and the Structure of Behavior* provides a clear report of the influence on the emerging field of cognitive psychology. Chomsky posited the distinction between performance and competence, offering the notion that variations in observed performance must be understood as generated by an underlying set of rules — grammatical competence — adequate to produce those variations. The logic of research involved detailed documentation of observable variation in language use, equally meticulous examination of language experience, and the *positioning* of a set of rules adequate to account for the differences between language that had been experienced and language that could be generated. The emphasis of contemporary sociolinguistics on a similar research paradigm is no coincidence.

As indicated earlier, these research programs are certainly not free of faults. Among the most serious has been the tendency to ignore the *substance* of classroom life, the specific curriculum content and subject matter being studied. One can read the meticulous detail of many classroom ethnographies and never discover the simple facts, concepts or principles, skills or understandings, being taught. One is overwhelmed with details of conversational alterations, body tonus modifications, distributions of speaking turns, patterns of individual and overlapping speech and chartings of pupil and teacher movements through the classroom. Even one of the leaders of the classroom ethnography field felt obliged to ask somewhat plaintively where were the stories of learning and teaching in ethnographic accounts of classrooms in a paper titled "Taught Cognitive Learning in Its Immediate Environment: A Neglected Topic in the Anthropology of Education" (Erickson, 1982b). Thus, for all of its emphasis on the particularities of context as the hallmark of research in the interpretive program, that context was defined by the research agenda of general sociolinguistics and microethnography which did not treat curriculum or instructional content as a core feature of context, as a feature worthy of characterization in detail. If process-product scholars were guilty of generalizing without due restraint across decontextualized molecular features of teaching processes, interpretive researchers were equally guilty of treating talk as talk, turns as turns, task as task, regardless of the subject matter under study by the participants.

Another problem of interpretive research lay in its commitment to the powerless, its strong tendency to locate its portrayal of personal meanings in the pupils in the classroom, especially those from ethnic or linguistic minorities, while often ignoring the perspective of teachers. While acknowledging that teachers, too, are often powerless in the school organization when compared to administrators or board members, in the ethnography of individual classrooms they become the oppressors or the tools of oppression, and the minority youngsters are the helpless victims. Too many of these portrayals thus present teachers as insensitive, uncaring, without skills or adequate understanding of the subtleties of cultural differences. The cognitive and emotional strain of teaching, the limits of teachers' capacities to respond to increasing complexity or diversity, the reasons why their behavior makes sense to them, all are likely to be ignored. The accounts are emic with respect to the pupils, but etic and even hostile in relation to the teacher. Here again, what is often a virtue of the interpretive program, an orientation toward seeing the world from the perspectives of those least likely to be understood in traditional research endeavors, becomes a liability with reference to the study of teaching.

There are at least two provisos to be offered in relation to this last criticism. First, a program should perhaps not be criticized for taking the interests of pupils as primary and those of teachers as secondary. Contemporary forms of a social history have injected a breath of fresh air into the study of history by supplementing with the heroic tales of white male politicians, business tycoons, and generals making power, money, and war with the history of women, minorities, and the poor. Similarly, a history of research on teaching that has portrayed classroom life only as seen by teachers might well be fruitfully enriched by new accounts providing the hitherto untold story of teaching from the perspective of the disadvantaged learner.

A second proviso emerges from the comment by Cadzen toward the end of her chapter in this volume. She speculates that the most useful kind of feedback to give teachers who have participated in research on discourse in their classrooms may well be accounts of what their pupils were doing, saying, thinking, and feeling, rather than detailed analyses of their own behavior. The portrayal of pupil responses to teaching may be more productive of positive changes in the teachers, and less likely to breed defensiveness and denial, than would descriptions of the teachers themselves. It is a researchable point and one worth taking seriously.

Finally, although the logic of inference and generalizability has attracted the attention of leaders in the interpretive program (e.g., Erickson, Heath) and although the tactics and strategies of data analysis, data reduction, and data use for inferences have now been examined in careful detail (Miles & Huberman, 1984), exemplars of this research program are far too often characterized by sloppy procedures, inadequate precision and control, and glib generalizations, from poorly and incompletely specified classroom particulars to assertions about the world of schools writ large. Geertz (1973) has observed:

> I have never been impressed by the argument that, as complete objectivity is impossible in these matters (as, of course, it is), one might as well let one's sentiments run loose. As Robert Solow has remarked, that is like saying that as a perfectly aseptic environment is impossible, one might as well conduct surgery in a sewer. (p. 30)

Research in the interpretive programs has injected a healthy note of criticism into the process–product-dominated conversations about teaching effectiveness. Now they must become concerned about the discipline of their own methods.

Teacher Cognition and Decision Making

The phrase "teacher behavior" rolls trippingly off the tongue. Those two words, *teacher* and *behavior*, have been paired almost automatically for many years in academic discussions of research on teaching, and even in more applied deliberations on teaching policy. When Gage defined research on teaching in the first *Handbook of Research on Teaching* as "research in which at least one variable consists of a behavior or characteristic of teachers" (Gage, 1963, p. 97), certainly no feelings of shock were elicited. Research was surely a process that involved the measurement and manipulation of *variables*, and an emphasis on behavior had been the cornerstone of American psychology since Watson. Since the studies of teacher characteristics, while certainly popular for many years, continued to produce few replicable findings, the emphasis fell increasingly on the description of what teachers did in the classroom, how their behavior related to student behavior, and how that behavior could best be shaped by training.

In Dunkin and Biddle (1974), teacher process variables were

at the very heart of the teaching model, and those process variables were composed of observable teacher behavior. What preceded and accompanied behavior were presage variables — for example, teacher characteristics — and context variables — for example, the subject matter, grade, or class size. Yet even as the research on teacher processes flourished, some scholars urged that other aspects of teaching, less immediately observable, more clearly associated with notions of thought, judgment, or decision making, be investigated. These researchers, such as Shavelson (1973) and Shulman and Elstein (1975), argued that the field of research on teaching was still embedded in a style of psychological language and theory that was already losing its hegemony in the behavioral sciences. Those disciplines were rapidly becoming "cognitive" in response to repeated demonstrations of the insufficiencies of behaviorist explanations. Yet research on teaching was being pursued as if teaching and thought were mutually incompatible. The only reference to teachers' thinking among all the studies cited in Dunkin and Biddle was an oblique one in their summary of Dahloff's (1971) and Lundgren's (1972) work on "steering groups."

The new emphasis on teacher cognition developed from several sources. First, beginning in the mid-1950s, the cognitive critique of behaviorism took hold in psychology, through the efforts of information-processing psychologists and psycholinguists. *Plans and the Structure of Behavior* (Miller et al., 1960) synthesized research and theory from the still-new fields of information-processing psychology (e.g., Newell & Simon, 1956) and transformational grammar (Chomsky, 1957) in a devastating critique of the adequacy of behaviorist explanations for complex human cognitive and skilled performance. During the same period, the work of Piaget, though dating back to the 1920s, first began to catch hold among American psychologists and educators. Translation of several of Piaget's later books, such as *The Origin of Intelligence in Children* (Piaget, 1952), brought the Swiss psychologist's work on cognitive development to the attention of an American audience now somewhat more sympathetic to his conceptions (if not yet to his methods). When Bruner, Goodnow, and Austin (1956) introduced notions of concept-attainment strategies and cognitive strain in their *Study of Thinking*, yet another legitimating study was added to the critique of behaviorism and the emergence of a new cognitive psychology. The trend was so powerful that, by the 1970s, one of the long-term leaders of behavioristic learning theory, Gregory Kimble (1975), observed:

> How far we have come in the past ten years; that the white rat and the pigeon no longer provide the majority of our data, that complex mazes are rarely used these days, that S-R has been deposed as king of the theoretical hill, that "mind" is no longer a dirty four-letter word. (p. 613)

It was no surprise then to find a generation of psychologists raised on the new information-processing and cognitive psychology beginning to train those lenses on the field of research on teaching. That field of research had certainly remained immune to the cognitive revolution Kimble found sweeping through psychology. The mental life of the teacher had not become a central topic of teaching research.

Shavelson (1983) has defined the purposes and rationale for this research program in the following manner:

> First, teachers are rational professionals who, like other professionals such as physicians, make judgments and carry out decisions in an uncertain, complex environment. ... teachers behave rationally with respect to the simplified models of reality they construct. ... teachers' behavior is guided by their thoughts, judgments and decisions. (pp. 392–393).

Therefore, to understand adequately the choices teachers make in classrooms, the grounds for their decisions and judgments about pupils, and the cognitive processes through which they select and sequence the actions they have learned to take while teaching, we must study their thought processes before, during, and after teaching.

Following Shulman and Elstein (1975), reviewers have tended to distinguish among three fundamental types of cognitive process research on teaching — studies of judgment and policy, of problem-solving, and of decision making. Each of the three genres of research presupposes a different form of task for teachers and a different type of research method for investigators. If anything, the influence of the psychological research models has been too strong, for they may have driven this program of research into a dead end.

Several strategic research sites have emerged in this program. Consistent with Jackson's (1968) distinction between preactive and interactive phases of teaching (roughly synonymous with planning and actively instructing, respectively) substantial research has focused on the cognitive processes observed in the course of teacher planning. Given the speed of normal classroom events, this strategy of studying the rare reflective moments during the life of a teacher was attractive. Thinking-aloud techniques were normally employed, with the teacher using his or her actual materials and/or planbook, or simulated materials prepared by the investigators. Protocols of the thinking aloud would be collected, perhaps followed by classroom observations and debriefing, perhaps not. The major research questions focused on descriptions of what teachers thought about as they planned for instruction, and the major finding identified most teachers as concentrating on content and activities in their planning, rather than formal objectives and individual characteristics of students. These findings regarding the contrast between current practices and the normative principles of planning typically espoused by instructional specialists constituted a serious indictment of conventional wisdom in teacher education. That is, if it is so clearly desirable to plan on the basis of considering the objectives of instruction and the characteristics of learners, why did no one practice that way?

A second major genre of research was the study of interactive thought, which had to employ methods of stimulated recall because thinking aloud is not possible in the conventional classroom while instruction is underway. Using video- or audiotapes of the classroom session recently completed, the participant is asked why he or she engaged in the observed behavior. Studies of interactive thought were far more difficult to conduct than were those of preactive teaching. The methods of stimulated recall had originally been developed by Bloom (1953) for study of student thought processes during college classes. They had been elaborated by Kagan, Krathwohl, and Miller (1963) for work with psychological counselors and subsequently, by Kagan, for work with other members of helping professions. Elstein and Shulman (with Kagan's collaboration) had applied the methods to the study of physician thought (e.g., Elstein, Shulman, & Sprafka, 1978; Shulman & Elstein, 1975). Chapters in this volume by Shavelson, Webb, and Burstein, as well as Clark and Peterson, discuss the methodological challenges of such techniques as thinking aloud and stimulated recall.

The forms taken in these studies varied enormously. In some studies (e.g., Peterson & Clark, 1978), preactive and interactive thinking was monitored for individual lessons during simulated microteaching sessions. The Alberta studies (e.g., MacKay & Marland, 1978) generally followed teachers in their actual classrooms for several days. Shroyer (1981) likewise studied interactive thought in teachers' natural classrooms for the duration of an entire unit of elementary mathematics. In his study of teacher planning, Yinger (1977) worked with the same teacher for nearly a year, again monitoring her actual second-grade classroom.

A third major genre of research used the methods of judgment and decision-making research to render mathematical models of teachers' cognitions about students. Shavelson and his students (Cadwell, Borko, Russo, Stern) applied the methods of "policy capturing" to model teacher judgments about pupils, using regression equations to represent the weights teachers implicitly gave to alternative sources of information in making decisions about pupil placements, evaluations, groupings, and the like.

Two serious problems beset the research program for the study of teacher cognitions. The first is the limited range of teaching activities about which teacher thoughts have been investigated. Other than the findings regarding teacher planning (findings that contrast observed planning emphases with those normative positions on teacher planning advocated by proponents of behavioral objectives and rational teaching models patterned after instructional design), little that is remarkable has emerged from the research studies. Moreover, most of the controversies among teacher cognition researchers themselves, such as the discussions over how many "real" decisions teachers make in a typical instructional hour, are of little practical or theoretical interest (unless one is only prepared to take teachers seriously as thinkers and professionals if it can be demonstrated that they make many decisions hourly rather than few). Most of the teaching activities have been tied closely to the process–product program, asking how teachers think about those behavioral performances identified as critical for effectiveness. These include assignments of pupils to groups, giving praise or criticism, setting and modifying pacing, allocating turns, and the like. These are important, and their importance will be discussed presently, but they represent a severely attenuated menu of teacher cognitions, a limited perspective on what it might be important for teachers to think about.

The second problem is the growing distance between the study of teacher cognition and those increasingly vigorous investigations of cognitive processes in pupils. The initial stimulus for research on cognition came from psychological approaches to the study of judgment, problem solving, and decision making. Models of research, ways of formulating questions, and general research paradigms were borrowed from previous psychological work in those areas. Thus studies of judgment policies in college admissions committees (Dawes, 1971) or of clinical problem solving in physicians (Elstein et al., 1978) established the templates for studies of cognition in teachers. But the central cognitive psychological work of the early 1970s was not the most important source of applications to the cognitive psychology of education in the late 1970s and the 1980s. Work in the psychology of instruction had moved toward the study of learning and problem solving in specific subject areas. Resnick (1981) summarizes the situation well in her chapter for the *Annual Review of Psychology*:

First, there is a shift toward studying more and more complex forms of cognitive behavior. This means that many of the tasks and processes of interest to cognitive psychologists are ones that can form part of a school's curriculum. Psychological work on such tasks is naturally relevant to instruction. Second ... is a growing interest in the role of *knowledge* in human behavior. Much effort is now directed at finding ways to represent the structure of knowledge and at discovering the ways in which knowledge is used in various kinds of learning.... Finally, today's assumptions about the nature of learning and thinking are interactionist. We assume that learning occurs as a result of mental constructions of the learner. These constructions respond to information and stimuli in the environment, but they do not copy or mirror them. This means that instruction must be designed not to put knowledge into learners' heads but to put learners in positions that allow them to construct well-structured knowledge. (p. 660)

Studies of the cognitive psychology of instruction concentrate on how students use their knowledge and conceptions to apprehend what they are taught. In the spirit of Herbart's (1895) conception of the appreciative mass, cognitive psychologists assume that all learners approach instruction actively.

They already possess extensive bodies of knowledge, organized in particular ways. When presented with new knowledge by texts or by teachers, they actively process the information in that instruction through the filters or lenses of their prior understanding.

The essential task for the teacher, therefore, is to appraise, infer, or anticipate these prior cognitive structures that students bring to the learning situation. Teachers must organize the content of their instruction in terms of those preconceptions, actively working to reveal and transform them when they would interfere with adequate comprehension of the new material to be taught. The language of this research program includes such key terms as *schema, script, frame, metacognitive strategy*, and other words to describe those mental tools or structures employed by learners to make sense of what they are being taught.

Quite centrally, the thrust of the cognitive research program in learning is subject matter specific rather than generic. That is, the schemata used to make sense of instruction on photosynthesis in a biology class are completely different from those used to understand the concept of inertia in physics.

With the exception of research programs of Leinhardt (e.g., 1983) and of Anderson and Smith (1984), most of the cognitive research on teaching has ignored the teacher's cognitive processes in this sense. There have been no studies of teachers' knowledge, of the schemata or frames they employ to apprehend student understandings or misconceptions.

Leinhardt's most recent work (e.g., Leinhardt & Smith, 1984) is exceptional in her application of the methods of cognitive science, not only to the representation of understanding in the minds of students, but also to the representation of and instruction in the same topics by the teachers. Classrooms are described in some detail and the cognitive understandings manifested by the participants, both teacher and students, are carefully mapped and analyzed.

Another interesting group of studies, deriving from roots in curriculum research and teacher education rather than cognitive psychology, has examined teachers' practical knowledge (e.g., Elbaz, 1981). In these studies, teachers are interviewed at length about their activities and choices, as well as the grounds for those choices. The researchers then develop a theory for practical pedagogical knowledge from the interview data and coordinated observations. This work is summarized by Feiman-Nemser and Floden (Handbook Ch. 18).

As intimated earlier, most others who study teacher thought have implicitly accepted the process–product model of teaching, as exemplified in the Dunkin–Biddle model, and have treated teachers' thoughts as processes that precede teacher behavior. Since the behavior in question is the same behavior deemed important in the process–product program, then the kinds of thoughts that are understood become those germane to the predominantly classroom-management behavior of teachers studied by that program.

Indeed, even the style of analysis resembles that of process–product research. Teachers are asked to think aloud while planning or to describe their thoughts and feelings during stimulated recall of interactive teaching. The resulting self-report protocols are then analyzed by counting the frequency of verbalizations under particular categories. Do teachers use objectives in planning? Count the relative frequency of references to objectives, activities, pupil characteristics, or specific content in the protocols and you have your answer: Teachers make very few references to objectives. How frequently do teachers make "in-flight" decisions during interactive instruction? Count the number of explicit decisions teachers recall making and you have your answer. The complexity and subtlety of cognitive science studies of learners is absent in such work, as are the theoretical constructs that make the cognitive psychology of instruction the most exciting single research program in educational psychology today.

There are, therefore, several kinds of cognitive studies of teachers being pursued. First, there are the studies of teachers' preactive and interactive thoughts in relation to the generic processes of teaching investigated by the process-product researchers. These are summarized and discussed by Clark and Peterson (Volume 3). Second, there are the studies of teachers' practical knowledge reviewed in this volume in the chapter by Feiman-Nemser and Floden. Research on subject matter understanding and representation by teachers as they instruct particular topics in specific subject matters is in its infancy. This work is closest in its orientation to the cognitive psychology of learning and will be discussed in greater detail presently. Additional studies of cognition in classrooms can be found in the work of the classroom process researchers employing sociolinguistic methods. Though they do not claim to be studying teacher cognition, much of their work throws significant light on how teachers and students jointly produce the rules of classroom life, and how teachers' understandings or misconstrual of the meanings communicated by children of different backgrounds can influence the choices teachers make and the interpretations and decisions they render.

A Missing Program. Where the teacher cognition program has clearly fallen short is in the elucidation of teachers' cognitive understanding of subject matter content and the relationships between such understanding and the instruction teachers provide for students (Shulman, 1984a). The general public and those who set educational policy are in general agreement that teachers' competence in the subjects they teach is a central criterion of teacher quality. They remain remarkably vague, however, in defining what sort of subject-matter knowledge they have in mind — basic skills, broad factual knowledge, scholarly depth — and the research-on-teaching community has been of little help with this matter.

In this discussion, I shall distinguish among three kinds of content knowledge: subject matter knowledge, pedagogical knowledge, and curricular knowledge. *Subject matter knowledge* is that comprehension of the subject appropriate to a content specialist in the domain. Thus it is the knowledge of physics expected of a successful university physics major, or the knowledge of Shakespeare's plays appropriate for a college English literature major. *Pedagogical knowledge* refers to the understanding of how particular topics, principles, strategies, and the like in specific subject areas are comprehended or typically misconstrued, are learned and likely to be forgotten. Such knowledge includes the categories within which similar problem types or conceptions can be classified (what are the ten most frequently encountered types of algebra word problems? least-well-grasped grammatical constructions?), and the psychology of learning them. *Curricular knowledge* is familiarity with the ways in which knowledge is organized and packaged for instruction, in texts, programs, media, workbooks, other forms of practice, and the like. It is the pedagogical equivalent of the physician's knowledge of *materia medica*, of the diversity of treatment alternatives.

How do we establish the state of these different forms of teaching knowledge? How much should teachers know, and about what? What are the consequences for teaching of different levels of these kinds of teaching knowledge? How are such forms of knowledge acquired from subject-matter courses in high school and in the subject-matter departments of the university? In professional education courses? From both supervised and unguided practical teaching experiences?

In a program of research only recently begun, my colleagues and I (Shulman, Sykes, & Phillips, 1983) are pursuing such questions. What are the sources of teacher explanations in particular instructional situations? When students have difficulty understanding a short story by Faulkner, or the principles of photosynthesis, where do teachers turn for their explanations, their examples, the analogies, metaphors, or similes employed to clarify the obscurity? Under what circumstances is depth of subject matter knowledge an apparent disadvantage to the teacher, and what strategies can remedy the problem? How does the character of the subject-matter knowledge possessed by teachers affect the cognitive quality of their teaching? How do different types of undergraduate subject-matter learning experiences in college result in different organizations of understanding for subsequent teaching? How do teachers approach the teaching of material they have never themselves learned before and how does this differ from their teaching of highly familiar material? How do teachers' general epistemic beliefs, their generic conceptions of knowledge, and their understanding of knowledge in their own discipline relate to the manner in which the subject is taught? In general, we are interested in examining in detail what most laypersons assume is the central question of teacher education. How much and what should teachers know of what they teach? Where is such knowledge acquired and how can it be improved or changed?

This research is pursued through a combination of oral intellectual histories, repeated interviews over a 1- to 2-year period of teacher education and beginning teaching, systematic observations of teacher planning, teaching, and retrospective assessment, analyses of simulated tasks involving the selection and critique of new teaching materials, and both observation and interviews in a variety of other settings.

One of the contentions of those who pursue research on teacher cognition has been that proper examination and reform of teacher education will be contingent upon progress in understanding teacher thought. This has certainly been the view of

Fenstermacher (1978) and others who have analyzed how re-search results can be used by teachers. Ironically, little is known about such matters empirically because these questions have fallen between the cracks in the research-on-teaching field. Nevertheless, new and emerging research programs, in which studies of teacher knowledge development are closely articulated with investigations of teacher education, promise to remedy those deficiencies in the coming years.

Although research on teacher cognition may have yielded less than was anticipated in its first decade, it remains an area of immense promise. Changes in both teaching and teacher education will become operational through the minds and motives of teachers. Understanding how and why teachers plan for instruction, the explicit and implicit theories they bring to bear in their work, and the conceptions of subject matter that influence their explanations, directions, feedback and correctives, will continue as a central feature of research on teaching. A comprehensive understanding of teaching will include explanations of both thought and action in teachers as well as students.

Summary and Prognosis

We come to the end of our discussion of the research programs in the study of teaching. The chapter began with a discussion of the concept of a research program and a clarification of how our treatment of this topic differed from the Kuhnian notion of a paradigm. The intrinsic incompleteness of social science research programs was discussed as well as some ways in which those insufficiencies might complement one another. That topic will be developed further in this section.

A synoptic map of the research-on-teaching field was then presented. It was schematic, necessarily leaving out important research initiatives. Programs were seen as making choices among a host of alternative units of inquiry for studying teaching. These units included *participants* (teacher, students, group-as-unit), *attributes* of those participants (capacities, thoughts, actions), *context* or levels of contextual aggregation (individual, group, class, school), *content* (topics, type of structure, duration of instructional unit), *agenda* (academic tasks, social organization) and foci within that agenda (subject matter content, participant structures), and *research perspective* (positivist/law-seeking or interpretive/personal meaning oriented). These choices resulted in strikingly different research programs, and hence strikingly different narratives about teaching, its antecedents and consequences.

Choices among research programs were not made so rationally, however. Investigations did not ponder the trade-offs among approaches and deliberately select that particular style of investigation that suited them optimally. Instead, they were driven by their individual disciplinary roots (and propensities within the discipline, as reflected in the differences between behaviorists and mentalists in psychology), their educational or political ideologies, their respective commitments to technical improvement or "scientific" explanation, and most of all, to the stage in which they became part of the Great Conversation. More than anything else, research programs were influenced by the dialogues and debates among scholars. Whether these occurred in print, in large national or regional meetings, or in the face-to-face sessions of invisible colleges, researchers reacted to each other's work. And since, in the modern era (since 1965), the process–product program represented the mainstream of research on teaching, it also served as the focal point for most of this conversation. Whether to elaborate and refine that model through specifying the influences mediating between process and product, or to demonstrate the putative insufficiency of the formulation, the other participants in the dialogue focused their attention on the mainstream approach. It became the most frequent source for guiding policymakers and teacher educators, and also the favorite target of critics from other perspectives in the field. It doubtless receives more than its fair share of criticism in this chapter as well.

The chapter continued with extensive discussions of the major research programs themselves, beginning with the process–product approach and continuing with a number of others. In portraying as members of a single program investigations that were distinguishable in significant ways, it did disservice to many studies and their authors. This is always the danger when the goal is broad classification and characterization. Moreover, there are doubtlessly significant portions of the research-on-teaching field that have been substantially ignored in this review, owing to lack of adequate understanding on my part.

In this final section of the chapter, I shall discuss a number of issues that cut across many of the programs discussed earlier.

These will include the types of knowledge produced in research on teaching, the conceptions of effectiveness implicit in different approaches, the role of ideology in the personal predilections of investigators for particular research programs, the contrasting implications for both educational policy writ large and teacher education in particular that flow from these research programs, and the conceptions of social science research and scientific progress that characterize the different programs.

I shall conclude the section with a discussion of the prognosis for the near future, with special reference to the search for "grand strategies" (Schwab, 1960/1978, pp. 220-225) that might overcome the limitations of the individual research programs we have reviewed.

Types of Knowledge

Different programs of research are likely to produce different types of knowledge about teaching, knowledge of interest to theoreticians, policymakers, and practitioners. There is no simple one-to-one correspondence between a particular research program and the knowledge produced within it. Moreover, in some research programs the knowledge is produced before any empirical work is conducted, and the empirical activities serve to test, refine, confirm, or elaborate the earlier conceptual work.

The following scheme is far from exhaustive, but is presented to suggest the range of types of knowledge to consider as we review the programs of research on teaching.

- *Empirical propositions.* These are generalizations that derive directly from empirical findings. They are most frequently found in discussions of process–product research, but can as easily be generated from research in any of the other programs. Examples include the most frequent statements of association in process–product work, for example, higher academic performance is associated with the use of ordered turns in first-grade reading groups.
- *Moral propositions.* These are normative generalizations that derive from value positions, ethical analyses, or ideological commitments. They frequently underlie other, ostensibly empirical analyses. For example, all the studies of teachers' expectation effects, whether conducted in the pro-

cess-product tradition or in the classroom ecology approach, rest on moral propositions regarding equity and equality of opportunity.

- *Conceptual inventions, clarifications, and critiques.* These are conceptual developments that may derive from empirical work, but involve a far longer leap from the data, or the inventive combining of empirical generalizations from diverse sources. Examples include Carroll's model of school learning, the concepts of direct instruction or active teaching, and Academic Learning Time. As Rosenshine has pointed out regarding the instructional technologies or protocols (to be discussed presently), these conceptual inventions do not derive directly from findings in any simple way. They are acts of scholarly imagination in which theoretical understanding, practical wisdom, and empirical generalizations are likely to combine into a more general formulation. The most important findings of Jackson's *Life in Classrooms* were a set of conceptual inventions (eg., preactive and interactive teaching) that were to enlighten much of research on teaching for the next decade.
- *Exemplars of practice or malpractice.* These are normally case descriptions of teachers, classrooms, or schools. They do not necessarily claim empirical generalizability. They are presented as instances or exemplars, documenting how education was accomplished (or stymied) by a particular group of teachers and students in a particular place. Florio's (1979) account of the teacher who taught writing through the creation of a simulated town, Erickson and Mohatt's (1982) descriptions of teaching in a North American Indian reservation school, or Smith and Geoffrey's (1968) analysis of teaching in a particular classroom are instances of this type.
- *Technologies or procedural protocols.* These are systematic approaches to instruction in which the sequence of desirable instructional events is specified. These include mastery learning, active mathematics teaching, and other procedural protocols described by Rosenshine and Stevens (this volume). Like conceptual inventions, they represent combinations of empirical generalization, practical experience, useful cases as exemplars, and the intuitions of a designer.

As indicated earlier, the types of knowledge do not map in a simple way onto the research programs. Both ethnographers and process-product researchers may offer empirical general-izations or conceptual inventions. Process-product researchers may even present case descriptions to exemplify aspects of their findings, though they are unlikely to present the personal inter-pretations of participants. Moral propositions are likely to lie undetected beneath most forms of research program.

Conceptions of Effectiveness

Contrasting conceptions of effectiveness accompany the differ-ent programs discussed in this chapter. All programs in which effectiveness was assessed as a function of empirically dem-onstrable relationships with academic achievement measures (or attitude scales, interest inventories, and the like) can be considered to employ *pragmatic* or *correlative* conceptions of effectiveness. Those practices or performances are effective that correlate with an outcome deemed desirable. This criterion of effectiveness is characteristic of both the teaching effectiveness and effective-schools approaches (Brophy & Good; Good & Brophy; Rosenshine & Stevens, all in this volume) to the study of teaching, as well as some more ethnographic studies of class-room process (e.g., Shulman, 1980).

A distinctive alternative is the *normative* conception of effec-tiveness, in which a given exemplar of instruction is compared to a model or conception of good teaching derived from a theory or ideology. This criterion of effectiveness uses *cor-respondence* rather than *correlation* as its test.

For example, Dewey argued that a central purpose of schools is to prepare citizens to function effectively in a democratic society. Therefore, classrooms and schools ought to be settings that, on inspection, provide opportunities for students to learn, the skills of democratic citizenship. One need not develop a test of democratic-skill outcomes to ascertain whether the oppor-tunities for participation, shared decision making, group delib-eration, and the like are presented. Flanders' (1970) research was initiated precisely for that reason, to study the extent to which the features of democratic societies were present in the typical classroom.

Effectiveness by correspondence can be found in many con-temporary studies of teaching as well. When Durkin (1981) studied the teaching of reading comprehension in elementary schools, she did not measure the effectiveness of observed in-struction against tests of reading comprehension. Instead, she began with an a priori normative model of reading comprehension instruction and used that as a template against which to measure the adequacy of the teaching and learning she observed. Similarly, when Erickson views the interactions between teacher and students, he uses a conception of effective teaching as accomplishing a match between the linguistic and cultural forms employed by the students and those encouraged, rewarded, and used by the teacher. His match/mismatch examination of classroom life uses an implicit normative criterion of effectiveness. These are both instances of effectiveness assessed by correspondence to a normative model rather than correlation with an empirical outcome.

It should be clear that no use of correlative criteria can be free of normative choices. Indeed, the selection of a particular empirical criterion instead of all other possibilities, the choice of a particular length of time or extensiveness of teaching episode as the unit of inquiry, all imply normative or value choices. Those who employ correlative criteria, such as standardized achievement tests, frequently avoid explicit consideration of the values or norms underlying their commitments. They must examine the outcome measures employed as indicators of product and determine whether *what* is measured adequately corresponds to the normative definitions of educational outcome to which they subscribe.

Similarly, those who would employ correspondence criteria must be prepared to demonstrate that the appearance of appropriate classroom organization, teacher explanations or instructional practices has been adequately documented. They may ultimately have to link their judgments of correspondence to claimed consequences of educational worth, whether in the form of measured student performance or predictions about the future character of a particular classroom or school. Thus, although pragmatic and normative criteria represent different approaches to judging the value of educational activities in the short run, a fully adequate program of research on teaching may well require the use of both kinds of assessment.

Unlike Dunkin and Biddle (1974), I do not encourage scholars to forego their normative commitments as they study teaching. Indeed, I find that the popularity of pragmatic or correlative criteria has too often led to mindless studies of teaching effectiveness. Especially when research begins once again (as it must) to study teaching in particular subject areas, conceptions of how knowledge ought to be represented in those areas will become central to judgments of effectiveness. Experts in those areas should not defer to existing standardized achievement tests as the appropriate criteria for measuring the adequacy of teaching. The tests should be adapted and modified until their measurements correspond to the judgment of experts in both the subject field and the cognitive psychology of learning.

Having devoted substantial attention to normative questions in the discussion of knowledge types and conceptions of effectiveness, we shall now turn to the role of ideology generally, as exemplified in the alternative ways scholars choose to study teaching.

Ideology

A number of the controversies reviewed earlier have rested on underlying differences of ideology. Some of these ideological differences are rooted in contrasting conceptions of education in general and teaching in particular; others around political commitments; yet others in relation to perspectives on proper forms of inquiry, whether dubbed scientific or not. Research programs are often adopted because of their consistency with favored ideological stances. Even more typically, programs are actively criticized or resisted because critics detect within them ideological implications the critics find offensive.

Dunkin and Biddle (1974) were critical of the tendency for researchers to employ their studies of teaching processes in the service of an ideological "commitment." They were particularly critical of the pioneering work of Flanders (e.g., 1970), whose commitment to the value of democratic classroom processes (in the spirit of Lewin, Lippitt, & White, 1939) lent a taint of advocacy to his research.

More recently, the ideological debates have swirled around the generic conflict between, broadly (and inaccurately) speaking, behaviorists and humanists. The humanists claim that process–product research and its Academic Learning Time offshoot derive from a "technological orientation" (e.g., Zumwalt, 1982) to both education and teaching. This orientation is said to focus on particular techniques or behaviors that can be practiced by teachers, leading to prescriptive standards of practice. Such standards "de-skill" the teaching profession, place undue emphasis on achievement gains as measured by standardized tests, and thereby render teaching merely technical rather than "deliberative" and require continuing decision making and artfulness by teachers.

Asserting that sin, like beauty, is often in the eye of the beholder, Gage (in press) argues that the search for lawful relationships between teaching and learning does not necessarily reflect a technological orientation, and surely does not inexorably lead to the teacher as robot. Indeed, reminding readers of his choice of title, "The Scientific Basis of the Art of Teaching" (Gage, 1978), he maintains that his perspective simply calls for the artful practice of teaching to be grounded in scientific propositions as much as possible, and surely not in technical maxims that have been substituted for pedagogical judgment.

Nevertheless, policies and programs for teacher selection and certification at the local and state levels have often taken the results of process–product research and translated them into rather inflexible evaluative standards (Shulman, 1983). Commissions have taken research on engaged time and prescribed longer school days or school years as a solution to low academic achievement. Contrary to the intentions of most leaders in the process–product program, the conception of teaching as a precisely prescribable set of behaviors for increasing pupil gain scores has flourished among designers of some teacher evaluation and staff development programs.

In teacher education, there has been a similar ideological conflict. Those who have pursued the program of teacher cognition and decision making have a strong commitment to a view of teaching as a profession populated by autonomous and learned professionals, much like medicine or law. Those whose studies have focused on the teaching career have generally shared that commitment to a body of research that will enhance teacher autonomy rather than restrict it. Hence, we can appreciate Zumwalt's (1982) unease with those process–product studies that incorporate "shoulds" for teachers into their experimental treatments or their statements of findings. The fact that such maxims are often commonplace in fields of medicine and law without doing great damage to their professionalism is rarely discussed. Ironically, however, it has been precisely the research programs that have been replete with such "shoulds" that have typically been found most valuable by those developing programs of professional development for experienced teachers, even from the vantage point of the teachers' unions (e.g., AFT, 1983).

I have not discussed research on teacher education or the teaching career thus far because it falls outside the bounds of the synoptic model presented earlier. I shall comment on the topic quite briefly at this point. *Teaching* is a beautifully ambiguous term. It describes a process engaged in by individuals in classrooms. That is the sense in which we have been using the term thus far in the chapter. But teaching is also the name for an occupation, a role that occupies the energies and commitments of many people over the course of their adult lives. Teaching is a set of understandings and skills, an occupation, a profession, a career. Teacher education is the process of being prepared to engage in the activities of that career.

We find in the study of teacher education and teaching a set of research programs roughly parallel to those already found in the study of classroom teaching. There are those who view teacher education from a process-product perspective and define research in teacher education as studies in which experimental treatments are manipulated with changes in teaching behavior seen as the outcomes. Others view teaching in the interpretive tradition and describe the experiences of being socialized into the teaching field from the perspectives of the initiates. Such is the work of Lacey (1977) in England, Zeichner (1983) and his colleagues in the United States, and many others whose work is presented by Lanier and Little (this volume).

Among those who study the occupation of teaching and the cultures that characterize it (Feiman-Nemser and Floden, this volume), there are those who treat the career as an unfolding, developmental pattern intrinsic to an occupation, following the traditions of professional socialization in medicine pioneered by Becker et al. (1961) and by Merton, Reader, and Kendall (1957). Others are much more attuned to the interaction between teachers and the particular organizational settings in which they work, concerned less with the universals of professional socialization than with the particulars of work in a context. Much of the work on the teaching profession falls into the interpretive/descriptive mode.

Conceptions of Social Science

At the heart of much of the debate over research programs have been differences in the fundamental conception of social science. This is not unique to the study of teaching. The world of social science and educational research has been rife with debates about the proper conceptions of inquiry in those fields. While the natural science models have dominated the first century of contemporary social science, severe doubts are now being expressed about the appropriateness of those models. Lee Cronbach (1975; 1982) has been among the most powerful of the critical voices. He has seriously questioned the separation of the social sciences from one another as well as from the humanities. He has called for a reduction in concern over methodological orthodoxies and urged that the most important criterion for good social research be the clarity with which it illuminates specific problems in particular contexts of both place and time. He raises serious doubts that inquiries disciplined by the experimental and quantitative procedures of the social sciences can lay claim to achieving significant levels of generalizability:

> All social scientists are engaged in case studies. The 1980 census is no less a case study than is Erikson's *Young Man Luther*. The observations take meaning from their time and place, and from the conceptions held by those who pose the questions and decide how to tabulate. (Cronbach, 1982, p.75)

In his characterization of social science research, Cronbach asserts that "social inquiry reports on events in one or more sites during one slice of time. It can be viewed as quantitatively assisted history" (Cronbach, 1982, p.74). This comparison between social science and educational research, on the one hand, and history on the other, is provocative. I have earlier remarked that I found the methodological catholicism of history, the manner in which a whole host of both disciplinary perspectives and methodological predilections can coexist in that one field of study, an important model for the study of teaching. In that spirit, I would like to consider some perspectives on the doing of history and consider their implications for our own work.

We have observed that a key feature distinguishing programs of research is their relative emphases on behavior or thought, on the observable and/or directly measurable actions and capacities of individuals or on the stated or inferred intentions, reasons, strategies, attitudes, feelings, expectations, goals or other cognitive states. The two emphases clearly connect to distinctive scholarly traditions.

One way to think about these two alternative perspectives, sometimes called the *etic* and the *emic* in the anthropology and the linguistic literatures, is through a discussion on the doing of history by one of our most eminent philosophers of history, R. G. Collingwood.

Collingwood (1946) contrasts the doing of history with the doing of natural science in a manner that highlights differences among researchers on teaching with regard to their perspectives on what kind of scholarship they pursue:

> The historian, investigating any event in the past, makes a distinction between what may be called the outside and the inside of an event. By the outside of the event I mean everything belonging to it which can be described in terms of bodies and their movements: the passage of Caesar, accompanied by certain men, across a river called the Rubicon at one date, or the spilling of his blood on the floor of the senate-house at another. By the inside of the event I mean that in it which can only be described in terms of thought: Caesar's defiance of Republican law, or the clash of constitutional policy between himself and his assassins, The historian is never concerned with either of these to the exclusion of the other. He is investigating not mere events (where by a *mere* event I mean one that has only an outside and no inside) but *actions*, and an action is the unity of the outside and inside of an event....
>
> In the case of nature, this distinction between the outside and the inside of an event does not arise. The events of nature are mere events, not the acts of agents whose thought the scientist endeavors to trace. It is true that the scientist, like the historian, has to go beyond the mere discovery of events; but the direction in which he moves is very different. Instead of conceiving the event as an action and attempting to rediscover the thought of its agent, penetrating from the outside of the event to its inside, the scientist goes beyond the event, observes its relation to others, and thus brings it under a general formula or law of nature. (pp. 213-214)

Collingwood's observations about the doing of history are instructive in two ways. They help us see more clearly the difference between the two research perspectives we have earlier distinguished, the positivist, law seeking, and the interpretive, meaning oriented. Additionally, Collingwood argues that, while distinctly different, the two approaches are not, in principle, incompatible. In fact, the proper work of the historian requires the commingling of the two orientations. This need to describe both events and their correlations as well as actions and their meanings is what makes history the fascinating methodological hybrid of the social sciences. (Or is it the humanities?)

Another question worth pursuing is whether the natural science perspective alone allows scholars to talk about "causes," while the interpretive researcher must be content to render explanatory accounts, that is, to tell compelling stories. Here again, Collingwood offers an insightful argument on the role of causal explanation in history:

> This does not mean that words like "cause" are necessarily out of place in reference to history; it only means that they are used there in a special sense. When a scientist asks "Why did that piece of litmus paper turn pink?" he means "On what kinds of occasions do pieces of litmus paper turn pink?" When an historian asks "Why did Brutus stab Caesar?" he means "What did Brutus think, which made him decide to stab Caesar?" The cause of the event, for him, means the thought in the mind of the person by whose agency the event came about: and this is not something other than the event, it is the inside of the event itself. (pp. 214–215)

Collingwood would thus argue that it is not only legitimate to combine the positivist and interpretive perspectives in the same field of study, it is an essential marriage in any truly comprehensive piece of historical (and, perhaps, educational) inquiry. We will examine some conceptions for combining such different approaches to research in the final section of this chapter.

Conceptions of Scientific Progress. Among many researchers, there is a view of scientific progress that we may call Newtonian, based on the observation often attributed to that great mathematician that if we can see far it is because we are as dwarfs standing on the shoulders of giants. (For an extraordinary discussion of the sources for that aphorism, see Merton, 1965.) In this view, science progresses additively, the work of more recent scholars aggregating with that of their predecessors to produce progress in scientific knowledge from generation to generation. The perspective is well expressed in a statement by Clark Hull (1943) describing the conditions for progress in learning theory:

> Progress...will consist in the laborious writing, one by one, of hundreds of equations; in the experimental determination, one by one, of hundreds of empirical constants contained in the equations; in the devising of practically usable units in which to measure the quantities expressed in the equations... in the rigorous deduction,

one by one, of thousands of theorems and corollaries from the primary definitions and equations; in the meticulous performance of thousands of critical quantitative experiments. (pp. 400–401)

This is a perspective on the cumulative character of scientific knowledge that fits well with the process–product program and its derivatives. Certainly the emphasis upon the meta-analysis of findings from disparate studies to establish empirical relationships more firmly is consistent with this view of cumulative progress. From this vantage point, it is difficult to understand how much of the research in the classroom ecology or teacher cognition programs can be construed as progressing, much less scientifically enlightening.

Kuhn's (1970) view of progress is quite different. Progress occurs as old paradigms are found wanting and new ones are invented to replace them. Often there are not adequate empirical grounds for choosing between competing paradigms. When a new paradigm emerges it often leaves behind, unanswered, many of the research questions that were at the heart of earlier paradigms. They are no longer critical puzzles. As Dewey (1898) observed in another context, speaking of the way in which Darwinist conceptions replaced the Aristotelian problem formulations that had preceded them, "we do not solve them; we get over them."

The sense of progress found in the work of interpretive researchers contrasts dramatically. Clifford Geertz (1973) expresses the view eloquently:

Cultural analysis is intrinsically incomplete. And, worse than that, the more deeply it goes the less complete it is. It is a strange science whose most telling assertions are its most tremulously based ...

The fact is that to commit oneself to ... an interpretive approach to the study of [culture] is to commit oneself to a view of ethnographic assertion as, to borrow W.B. Gallie's by now famous phrase, "essentially contestable." Anthropology, or at least interpretive anthropology, is a science whose progress is marked less by perfection of consensus than by a refinement of debate. What gets better is the precision with which we vex each other. (p. 29)

To the extent that this sense of progress indeed characterizes the work of those who conduct interpretive research on teaching, the ideological conflict regarding the goals and functions of science becomes clear. It is also apparent why the results of positivist research are more typically employed to guide policy while those of interpretive researchers most frequently are employed to criticize and question, to vex with precision.

This becomes a source of great frustration for policymakers who want research to point the way to correct practices and procedures. Kenneth Prewitt (quoted in Cronbach, 1982) attempted to alleviate those frustrations (though not entirely to relieve them) in his testimony before the House Subcommittee on Science, Research, and Technology:

> The complexities of the problems for which the social and behavioral sciences might be helpful are always going to be one step ahead of the problem-solving abilities of those sciences.... They are sciences whose progress is marked, and whose uesfulness is measured, less by the achievement of consensus or the solving of problems than by a refinement of debate and a sharpening of the intelligence upon which collective management of human affairs depend. (p.75)

Views of Teaching and Teacher Education

How can these alternative perspectives on the study of teaching be resolved? How can we be guided with respect to what constitutes the knowledge base of teaching and how it grows? What does a teacher need to know and to do in order to function well? And how does that knowledge relate to the results of research on teaching? Agreeing with Gage (1978) and others, Schwab (1983) defines teaching as an art. He proceeds to discuss the characteristics of an art:

> Every art, whether it be teaching, stone carving or judicial control of a court of law...has rules, but knowledge of the rules does not make one an artist. Art arises as the knower of the rules learns to apply them appropriately to the particular case. Application, in turn, requires acute awareness of the particularities of that case and ways in which the rule can be modified to fit the case without complete abrogation of the rule. In art, the form must be adapted to the matter. Hence the form must be communicated in ways which illuminate its possibilities for modification. (p. 265)

If teaching is an art, its practice requires at least three different forms of knowledge: These are knowledge of rules of principles, knowledge of particular cases, and knowledge of ways to apply appropriate rules to properly discerned cases. Most successful process-product research produces propositional rules. Such general rules include propositions about assigning praise or blame, allocating turns, sequencing instruction, checking for understanding, and the like (see Rosenshine & Stevens, this volume). There are also general maxims that do not necessarily derive from research on teaching, but are part of the traditional wisdom of the practitioner.

In this regard, medicine is often proposed as a proper model for education. The results of basic and clinical medical research provide general principles that guide clinical choices in particular circumstances (or at least indicate that the practice should be consistent with those principles). Medical students learn that portion of the knowledge base during their premedical and pre-clinical education. They then proceed to clinical clerkships and graduate residency education to acquire knowledge of cases and opportunities for supervised practice in applying rules to such cases.

The ambiguity of the term "case" can be problematic. In teaching, the term not only represents types of individual children (the typical referent for a "case" study), but also types of classrooms or schools, and types of subject-matter content to be taught. These elements would produce many conjunctions of child, class, and subject. I use "types" purposely since I do not view cases as unique events, but as instances of a broader class. To call something a case is to make the claim that it is a "case of something." Even in an idiographic enterprise, cases must have some generalizability or their potential value in the knowledge base is severely limited.

An alternative to the medicine-like view of the knowledge base of teaching may be the analogy of law and legal practice. In medicine, the claim is that the general propositions derive from scientific processes of observation, experimentation, inter- petation, and generalization — the use of empirical methods of inductive inquiry. The general rules then act in the manner of major premises from which clinical practices are deduced, as mediated by observations of particular circumstances that serve as minor premises. In law, however, there is no body of empiri- cally demonstrated generalizations forming the knowledge base of the field. Instead, there are general normative principles deal- ing with such generic concepts as justice, property, individual rights, and social obligations, These typically take the form of laws, regulations, or statutes. Legal education is a process of learning to find one's way through the thicket of documented cases to find proper precedents for the current problem. Instead of reasoning deductively from general principles to particular cases, the attorney or judge typically reasons analogically from other cases *qua* precedents to the particularities of the case at hand. Alternative candidates for the status of precedent are weighed in light of the features of the present case and in regard to the normative principles germane to the case until a justifiable judgment or decision can be rendered. That judgment is then entered into the cumulative record that aggregates into the body of case law. Learning the knowledge base of law requires repeated opportunities to practice the classification and retrieval of cases and the analogical combining of rules and cases.

An image of the teaching art such as this one is provocatively parallel to that of Fenstermacher (1978). Following Green (1971), Fenstermacher argues that educating a teacher is not a matter of inculcating a knowledge base in the form of a specific set of teaching skills and competencies. Rather, to educate a teacher is to influence the premises on which a teacher bases practical reasoning about teaching in specific situations. In Green's terms, these are the premises of the practical argument in the mind of the teacher. These premises are derived, in part, from the generalizations of empirical research on teaching. The premises serve to ground the decisions, not determine them.

Yet another analogy can be drawn to architecture, where the practitioner simultaneously derives guidance from two bodies of knowledge, the physics, mathematics, and chemistry of engineering and materials science and the accumulated wealth of cases from the Acropolis to the Transamerica Building, from a Navajo Indian village to Levittown. The scientific principles of construction, heating, lighting, and the like will progress in a Newtonian or Kuhnian manner. In that sense, Frank Lloyd Wright had a larger-principled knowledge base than Sir Christopher Wren, as did Mies van der Rohe relative to Bramante. But the accumulated exemplars of architectural design form the case literature for practitioners. (See Soltis, 1975, for a similar analysis.)

In all these senses, we can view the study of teaching progressing. Both our scientific knowledge of rules and principles (properly construed as grounds, not prescriptions) and our knowledge of richly .described and critically analyzed cases combine to define the knowledge base of teaching. The guided and supervised practice needed to learn how to apply, adapt, and, when necessary, invent rules for particular cases understood as instances of classes of events, that practice constitutes another component of the knowledge base. And this base must incorporate rules and cases for subject matter content and its pedagogy as well as for the organization and management of instruction.

While it has been inspiring to state the case for learning from cases, the fact is that we have little idea of how such a process works. How do practitioners learn vicariously from the documented experiences of others? We know from the literature on human judgment and decision making (e.g., Tversky & Kahneman, 1974; Nisbett & Ross, 1980) that most individuals find specific cases more powerful influences on their decisions than impersonally presented empirical findings, even though the latter constitute "better" evidence. Although principles are powerful, cases are memorable, and lodge in memory as the basis for later judgments. But why this is the case, and how to make this kind of process work to the advantage of reflection and intelligent practical reasoning, rather than as one of the "idols of the mind" (Bacon, 1620), is a serious problem for those who study the education of teachers.

Search for a Grand Strategy

If any one program of research is in principle insufficient, is there no alternative to conducting research that is limited in its perspectives or applications? Schwab (1960, 1978) has discussed this as the question or a "grand strategy" (1978, pp. 220–221). Having dismissed the possibility of any one strategy being best, Schwab (1978) asserts that a circumstance much like we confront in research on teaching may well be a blessing rather than a sign of weakness:

> We need not, therefore, *make* a virtue of the necessity of pursuing enquiry through men who are moved by numerous preferences to work in different ways toward differing specifications of their common goal. It *is* a virtue.
>
> Yet, as long as resources for research are limited, there is an itch to believe that one of the several strategies available to science is the best one.... I have tried to show that this hope must betray us. Consensus on a single pattern of choices will merely enable us to overlook what we have not done in our enquiry.... This leaves the

possibility that some particular *order* of different strategies, consti-
tuting a grand strategy, may be better than all other orders. (p.221)

Several researchers on teaching have advocated versions of a
grand strategy. The most popular of these is the "descriptive-
correlational-experimental loop." Gage (1978) among others
has advocated an order of studies in which general qualitative
description of a small number of cases is the first stage of research. After important variables and constructs have been
identified using those descriptive studies (exemplars leading to
conceptual inventions), large-scale process–product correlational studies are conducted to identify discrete relationships
between individual teacher behaviors and student outcomes at
a level of specificity and precision unavailable through qualitative work (leading to empirical generalizations). Scholars then
organize the array of empirical generalizations into composites
(more conceptual invention) for purposes of field testing. The
last stage of research is controlled experimentation to establish
causal links between those composite models of teaching (now
in the form of instructional technologies or teaching protocols)
and student learning outcomes. Gage (in press) maintains that
this has been the pattern followed in the successful process–product program. Moreover, he urges that the descriptive–correlational–experimental loop become the basis for a new era of
collaboration between those involved in process–product work
and those in the ethnographic/sociolinguistic program.

Another view of grand strategy moves in exactly the opposite
direction from the descriptive-correlational-expermental loop.
Ethnographers such as Erickson (Volume 2) have argued that the
empirical propositions emanating from procewss-product work
are too general to provide adequately concrete guidance to
teachers unless they are followed by much more thickly described interpretive work. Thus Erickson claims that any stage
of generalization, whether produced through correlational
studies or experiments, must be followed by the particularization
of concrete detail characteristic of classroom ethnographies.
Both arguments appear sound. Two alternative grand strategies
have been proposed, and each will be germane under the correct
circumstances. How might we think about such circumstances?

Evertson and Green (Handbook Ch. 6) advocate thinking aout
observational research on teaching in terms of programs of
research that blend approaches traditionally labeled quantitative

or qualitative as appropriate for the particular phenomena under investigation. They provide extremely useful heuristics for determining how to combine methods of observation in a sequence of studies forming a program of research.

Cronbach (1982) also argues for an eclectic strategy:

> What research styles and objectives follow from the intent to advance understanding? A mixed strategy is called for: censuses and laboratory experiments, managerial monitoring and anthropological *Einfühlung*, mathematical modeling and unstructured observation. A few maxims can be offered even for eclectic social science. (p. 73)

Although Cronbach's call for eclecticism is one with which I can surely resonate in principle, the practice of such combined strategies is complex indeed. One of the strategies more frequently encountered these days could best be called the "goulash" or "garbage can" approach. It is a form of eclecticism run wild, with little or no discipline to regulate the decisions. In these studies, many forms of research are incorporated and thrown together with little thought for the differences in their purposes, assumptions, or perspectives. Systematic observations are conducted randomly throughout the year for thirty minutes each as is typical for the process-product study. Case studies of particular classes are thrown in for purposes of "thick description," but nothing about the resulting descriptions is either thick or interpretively descriptive. They are simply impressionistic descriptions written in the etic style of process-product research, but without its characteristic precision. Undisciplined eclecticism is no virtue when compared to carefully conducted research within a particular research program's tradition. Indeed, it is probably worse.

Nevertheless, we need not give up on the notion of research programs conducted in the spirit of disciplined eclecticism. A new generation of educational scholars is being prepared who are truly research methodologists, that is, capable of employing alternative approaches to problems as they are formulated, rather than the orthodox research methodists of an earlier generation (Shulman, 1984b). Moreover, the development of research centers and institutes in which representatives of distinctly different research programs and traditions can work collaboratively shows promise for the development of healthy new hybrid programs. It may be that in many cases individual studies cannot be pursued jointly; the canons of each research program must be allowed to function, thus to discipline the inquiry as it is pursued. But when investigators have learned to speak each other's languages, to comprehend the terms in which other programs' research questions are couched, then processes of deliberation over findings can yield the hybrid understandings not possible when members of individual research programs dwell in intellectual ghettos of their own construction.

With respect to the concept of a grand strategy, my own view is that, while the concept is heuristically useful, there exists no particular sequence or order of approaches that is generally optimal. The order selected will reflect the particular propensities or styles of the investigators, the ways in which the research problem is cast as influenced by prior research or by policy issues. Most important, the order will be determined by the dialogue in the Great Conversation, with the excitement engendered or horror elicited by recently conducted pieces of research. The responses they elicit from among other members of the research community will determine which studies are appropriate to pursue next.

Zumwalt (1982, pp. 232–233) reported that after the excitement associated with publication of the first *Handbook of Research on Teaching*, authors for the *Second Handbook* found little to crow about. Travers, editor of the 1973 volume, observed that "those who participated in the first *Handbook* would never have guessed that, a decade later, authors of the *Second Handbook* would be having even greater difficulty in finding significant research to report than did their predecessors" (Travers, 1973, pp. vii–viii).

This is certainly not the case some 12 years later as we examine the present third edition. Findings have proliferated. Many have been replicated and extended. Policymakers and practitioners alike take the research seriously and apply its results to their activities. No contemporary field of applied social science research has attracted the range and diversity of disciplinary efforts in the pursuit of its questions as has research on teaching. The absence of a single research paradigm is not a sign of pathology in the field. The presence of active, occasionally even acrimonious, debate among investigators does not signal danger for the field of study. The publication of this edition finds research on teaching in a state of admirable vigor and promising progress. It is not Newtonian progress, to be sure, but it is precisely the kind of development appropiate to educational inquiry. Its benefits are manifold for they promise to lead to a deeper theoretical understanding of teaching, a continuing documentation of its many forms and functions, and the likelihood of more enlightened future approaches to the entire teaching enterprise.

REFERENCES

American Federation of Teachers. (1983). Final Report, Research Dissemination Project. Washington, DC: National Institute of Education.

Anderson, C., & Smith, E. (1984). Children's preconceptions and content-area textbooks. In G. Duffy, L. Roehler, & J. Mason (Eds.), *Comprehension instruction: Perspectives and suggestions.* New York: Longman.

Anderson, L. (1984). The environment of instruction: The function of seatwork in a commercially developed curriculum. In G. Duffy, L. Roehler, & J. Mason (Eds.), *Comprehension instruction: Perspectives and suggestions.* New York: Longman.

Anderson, L., Evertson, C., & Brophy, J. (1979). An experimental study of effective teaching in first-grade reading groups. *Elementary School Journal, 79*(4), 193–223.

Anderson, L., Evertson, C., & Emmer, E. (1980). Dimensions of classroom management derived from recent research. *Journal of Curriculum Studies, 12*, 343–356.

Armbruster, B. B., Stevens, R. J., & Rosenshine, B. (1977). *Analyzing content coverage and emphasis: A study of three curricula and two tests* (Tech. Rep. No. 26). Urbana–Champaign: University of Illinois, Center for the Study of Reading.

Au, K. (1980). Participation structures in a reading lesson with Hawaiian children. *Anthropology and Education Quarterly, 11*(2), 91–115.

Bacon, F. (1902). *Novum organum.* (J. Dewey, Ed.). New York: P. F. Collier. (Original work published 1620).

Barr, R., & Dreeben, R. (1978). Instruction in classrooms. In L. S. Shulman (Ed.), *Review of research in education* (Vol. 5). Itasca, IL: F. E. Peacock.

Barr, R., & Dreeben, R. (1983a). *How schools work.* Chicago: University of Chicago Press.

Barr, R., & Dreeben, R. (1983b). School policy, production, and productivity. In L. S. Shulman & G. Sykes (Eds.), *Handbook of teaching and policy.* New York: Longman.

Becker, H. S., Geer, B., & Hughes, E, (1968). *Making the grade: The academic side of college life.* New York: John Wiley.

Becker, H. S., Geer, B., Hughes, E., & Strauss, A. (1961). *Boys in white:*

Student culture in medical school. Chicago: University of Chicago Press.

Bennett, N., Jordan, J., Long, G., & Wade, B. (1976). *Teaching styles and pupil progress.* Cambridge MA: Harvard University Press.

Berliner, D. C. (1979). Tempus educare. In P. L. Peterson and H. J. Walberg (Eds.), *Research on teaching.* Berkeley, CA: McCutchan.

Bloom, B. S. (1953). Thought-processes in lectures and discussions. *Journal of General Education, 7*(3), 160–169.

Bloom, B. S. (1968). Learning for mastery. *Evaluation comment.* UCLA—CSEIP, 1, n.p.

Bloom, B. S. (1976). *Human characteristics and school learning.* New York: McGraw-Hill.

Brophy, J. E. (1983). Classroom organization and managment. *Elementary School Journal, 83*(4), 265–286.

Brophy, J. E., & Good, T. L. (1974). *Teacher-student relationships: Causes and consequences.* New York: Holt, Rinehart and Winston.

Bruner, J. S., Goodnow, J. J., & Austin, G. A. (1956). *A study of thinking.* New York: John Wiley.

Carroll. J .B. (1963). A model for school learning. *Teachers College Record, 64*(8), 723–733.

Chomsky, N. (1957). *Syntactic structures.* Hawthorne, NY: Mouton.

Clark, C. M., & Yinger, R. J. (1979). Teacher thinking. In P. L. Peterson & H. J. Walberg (Eds.), *Research on teaching.* Berkeley, CA: McCutchan.

Coleman, J. S., Campbell, E. Q. Hobson, C. J.. McPartland, J. Mood, A. M., Weinfeld, F. D., & York, R. L. (1966). *Equality of educational opportunity.* Washington, D.C.: U.S. Government Printing Office.

Collingwood, R. G. (1946). *The idea of history.* New York: Oxford University Press.

Cronbach, L. J. (1975). Beyond the two disciplines of scientific psychology. *American Psychologist, 30*(2), 116–127.

Cronbach, L. J. (1982). Prudent aspirations for social inquiry. In L. Kruskal (Ed.), *The future of the social sciences.* Chicago: University of Chicago Press.

Dahloff, U. (1971). *Ability grouping, content validity, and curriculum process analysis.* New York: Teachers College Press, Columbia University.

Dawes, R. M. (1971). A case study of graduate admissions: Application of three principles of human decision making. *American Psychologist, 26*(2), 180–188.

Delamont, S., & Atkinson, P. (1980). The two traditions in educational ethnography: Sociology and anthropology compared. *British Journal of Sociology of Education, 1*, 139–152.

Dewey, J. (1910). The influence of Darwinism on philosophy. In J. Dewey, *The influence of Darwinism on philosophy, and other essays.* New York: H. Holt & Co. (Original work published 1898).

Doyle, W. (1977). Learning the classroom environment: An ecological analysis. *Journal of Teacher Education, 28*, 51–55.

Doyle, W. (1978). Paradigms for research on teacher effectiveness. In L. S. Shulman (Ed.), *Review of research in education* (Vol 5). Itasca, IL: F. E. Peacock.

Doyle, W. (1983). Academic work. *Review of Educational Research, 53*(2), 159–199.

Doyle, W. (in press). Paradigms for research on teaching. In T. Husen and T. N. Postlethwaite (Eds.), *International encyclopedia of education: Research and studies.* Oxford: U.K.: Pergamon.

Dunkin, M. J., & Biddle, B. J. (1974). *The study of teaching.* New York: Holt, Rinehart and Winston.

Durkin, D. (1981). Reading comprehension instruction in five basal reading series. *Reading Research Quarterly,* 16(4), 515–544.

Elbaz, F. (1981). The teacher's "practical knowledge": Report of a case study. *Curriculum Inquiry,* 7(1), 43–71.

Elstein, A. S., Shulman, L. S., & Sprafka, S. A. (1978). *Medical problem solving: An analysis of clinical reasoning.* Cambridge, MA: Harvard University Press.

Emmer, E., Evertson, C., & Anderson, L. (1980). Effective classroom management at the beginning of the school year. *Elementary School Journal, 80,* 219–231.

Erickson, F. (1973). What makes school ethnography ethnographic? *Council of Anthropology and Education Newsletter, 2,* 10–19.

Erickson, F. (1982a). Classroom discourse as improvisation: Relationships between academic task structure and social participation structures in lessons. In L. C. Wilkinson (Ed.), *Communicating in the classroom.* New York: Academic Press.

Erickson, F. (1982b). Taught cognitive learning in its immediate environment: A neglected topic in the anthropology of education. *Anthropology and Education Quarterly, 13,* 149–180.

Erickson, F., & Mohatt, G. (1982). Cultural organization of participant structures in two classrooms of Indian students. In G. D. Spindler (Ed.), *Doing the ethnography of schooling: Educational anthropology in action.* New York: Holt, Rinehart and Winston.

Evertson, C., Emmer, E., Sanford, J., & Clements, B. (1983). Improving class management: An experiment in an elementary classroom. *Elementary School Journal, 84*(2), 173–188.

Fenstermacher, G. D. (1978). A philosophical consideration of recent research on teacher effectiveness. In L. S. Shulman (Ed.), *Review of research in education, Vol. 6* (pp. 157–185). Itasca, IL: F. E. Peacock.

Feyerabend, P. (1974). How to be a good empiricist—A plea for tolerance in matters epistemological. In P. H. Nidditch (Ed.), *The philosophy of science* (pp. 12–39). Oxford: Oxford University Press.

Fisher, C., Filby, N., Marliave, R., Cahen, L., Dishaw, M., Moore, J., & Berliner, D. (1978, June). *Teaching behaviors, academic learning time, and student achievement. Beginning teacher evaluation study* (Phase III-B, final report). San Francisco: Far West Labotatory.

Flanders, N. A. (1970). *Analyzing teacher behavior.* Reading, MA: Addison-Wesley.

Florio, S. (1978). *Learning how to go to school.* Unpublished doctoral dissertation, Harvard University.

Florio, S. (1979). The problem of dead letters: Social perspectives on the teaching of writing. *Elementary School Journal, 80*(1), 1–7.

Freeman, D. J., Kuhs, T. M., Knappen, L. B., Floden, R. E., Schmidt, W. H., & Schwille, J. R. (1983). Do textbooks and tests define a natural curriculum in elementary school mathematics? *Elementary School Journal, 83*(5), 501–514.

Gage, N. L. (Ed.), (1963). *Handbook of research on teaching.* Chicago: Rand McNally.

Gage, N. L. (1978). *The scientific basis of the art of teaching.* New York: Teachers College Press, Columbia University.

Gage, N. L. (in press). Hard gains in the soft sciences: The case of pedagogy. *Phi Delta Kappa Monographs.*

Gage, N. L. & Giaconia, R. (1981). Teaching practices and student achievement: Causal connections. *New York University Education Quarterly, 12*(3), 2–9.

Gagné, R. M. (1970). *The conditions of learning* (2nd ed.). New York: Holt, Rinehart, and Winston.

Geertz, C, (1973). Thick description: Toward an interpretive theory of culture. In C. Geertz, *The interpretation of cultures* (pp. 3–30). New York: Basic Books.

Geertz, C. (1983). Blurred genres: The refiguration of social thought. In C. Geertz, *Local knowledge.* New York: Basic Books.

Glaser, R. (Ed.), (1962). *Training research and education.* Pittsburgh: University of Pittsburgh Press.

Good, T. L. (1979). Teacher effectiveness in the elementary school: What we know about it now. *Journal of Teacher Education, 30,* 52–64.

Good, T. L. (1983). Classroom research: A decade of progress. *Educational Psychologist, 18*(3), 127–144.

Good, T. L., Biddle, B. J. & Brophy, J. E. (1975). *Teachers make a difference.* New York: Holt, Rinehart and Winston.

Good, T. L., Grouws, D. A., & Beckerman, T. (1978). Curriculum pacing: Some empirical data in mathematics. *Journal of Curriculum Studies, 10*(1), 75–82.

Good, T. L., Grouws, D. A., & Ebmeier, H. (1983). *Active mathematics teaching.* (Research on Teaching Monograph Series). New York: Longman.

Green, J. L. (1983). Teaching and learning: A linguistic perspective. *Elementary School Journal, 83*(4), 353–391.

Green, T. F. (1971) *The activities of teaching.* New York: McGraw-Hill.

Hamilton, S. F., (1983). The social side of schooling: Ecological studies of classrooms and schools. *Elementary School Journal, 83*(4), 313–334.

Harnischfeger, A., & Wiley, D. E. (1976). The teaching–learning process in elementary schools: A synoptic view. *Curriculum Inquiry, 6*(1), 5–43.

Heath, S. B. (1983). *Ways with words.* Cambridge: Cambridge University Press.

Herbart, J. F. (1895). *The science of education, its general principles deduced from its aim and the aesthetic revelation of the world* (Trans. from German by Herluf & Emme Felkin). Boston: D. C. Heath.

Hull, C. L. (1943). *Principles of behavior.* New York: Appleton.

Jackson, P. W. (1968). *Life in classrooms.* New York: Holt, Rinehart & Winston.

Kagan, N., Krathwohl, D. R., & Miller, R. (1963). Stimulated recall in therapy using video tape — a case study. *Journal of Counseling Psychology, 10*(3), 237-243.

Kimble, G. A. (1975). Required reading for the profession [Review of E. Hilgard & G. Bower, *Theories of learning* (4th ed.)]. *Contemporary Psychology, 20*(8), 613-614.

Kounin, J. (1970). *Discipline and group management in classrooms.* New York: Holt, Rinehart & Winston.

Kuhn, T. S. (1970). *The structure of scientific revolutions* (2nd ed. enlarged). Chicago: University of Chicago Press. (Original work lished 1964).

Lacey, C. (1977) *The socialization of teachers.* London: Methuen.

Lakatos, I. (1970). Falsification and the methodology of scientific research programmes. In I. Lakatos & A. Musgrave (Eds.) *Criticism and the growth of knowledge.* Cambridge: Cambridge University Press.

Leinhardt, G. (1983). Novice and expert knowledge of individual students' achievement. *Educational Psychologist, 18*(3), 165-179.

Leinhardt, G., & Smith, D. (1984, April). Expertise in mathematics instruction: Subject-matter knowledge. Paper presented at the annual meeting of the American Educational Research Association, New Orleans.

Lewin, K., Lippitt, R., & White, R. (1939). Patterns of aggressive behavior in experimentally created "social climates." *Journal of Social Psychology, 10*, 271-299.

Lightfoot, S. L. (1983). *The good high school.* New York: Basic Books.

Lundgren, U. P. (1972). *Frame factors and the teaching process: A contribution to curriculum theory and theory on teaching.* Stockholm: Almgrist and Wiksell.

MacKay, A., & Marland, P. (1978). Thought processes of teachers. Presented at the meeting of the American Educational Research Association, Toronto.

Masterman, M. (1970). The nature of a paradigm. In I. Lakatos & A. Musgrave (Eds.), *Criticism and the growth of knowledge.* Cambridge: Cambridge University Press.

McDermott, R. P. (1976). *Kids make sense: An ethnographic account of the interactional management of success and failure in one first-grade classroom.* Unpublished doctoral dissertation, Stanford University, Stanford, CA.

McDonald, F., & Elias, P. (1976). *The effects of teacher performance on pupil learning. Beginning teacher evaluation study* (Phase II, final report, Vol. I). Princeton, NJ: Educational Testing Service.

Mehan, H. (1979). *Learning lessons: Social organization in the classroom.* Cambridge, MA: Harvard University Press.

Merton, R. K. (1959). Notes on problem finding in sociology. In R. K. Merton, L. Broom, & L. S. Cottrell, Jr. (Eds.), *Sociology today* pp. ix-xxxiv. New York: Basic Books.

Merton R. K. (1965). *On the shoulders of giants: A Shandean postscript.* New York: The Free Press.

Merton, R. K. (1967). On sociological theories of the middle range. In R. K. Merton, *On theroretical sociology* pp. 39-72. New York: The Free Press.

Merton, R. K. (1975). Structural analysis in sociology. In P. Blau (Ed.), *Approaches to the study of social structure*. New York: The Free Press.

Merton, R. K., Reader G. G., & Kendall, P. (Eds.). (1957). *The student physician: Introductory studies in the sociology of medical education*. Cambridge, MA: Harvard University Press.

Miles, M. B., & Huberman, A. M. (1984). *Qualitative data analysis: A sourcebook of new methods*. Beverly Hills: Sage Publications.

Miller, G. A., Galanter, E., & Pribram, K. H. (1960). *Plans and the structure of behavior*. New York: Holt, Reinhart & Winston.

Mitzel, H. E. (1960). Teacher effectiveness. In C. W. Harris (Ed.), *Encyclopedia of educational research* (3rd ed., pp. 1481–1486). New York: Macmillan.

Newell, A., & Simon, H. A. (1956). The logic theory machine: A complex information processing system. *I.R.E. Transactions on information theory, 2*, 61–79.

Nisbett, R. E., & Ross, L. (1980). *Human inference: Strategies and shortcomings of social judgement*. Englewood Cliffs, NJ: Prentice-Hall.

Peshkin, A. (1978). *Growing up American: Schooling and the survival of community*. Chicago: University of Chicago Press.

Peterson, P. L., & Clark, C. M. (1978). Teachers' reports of their cognitive processes during teaching. *American Educational Research Journal, 15*(4), 555–565.

Peterson, P. L., & Swing, S. R. (1982). Beyond time on task: Students' reports of their thought processes during classroom instruction. *Elementary School Journal, 82*(5), 481–491.

Phillips, S. U. (1983). *The invisible culture: Communication in classroom and community on the Warm Spring Indian Reservation*. New York & London: Longman.

Piaget, J. (1952). *The origin of intelligence in childen*. New York: International Universities Press.

Resnick, L. B. (1981). Instructional psychology. *Annual Review of Psychology, 32*, 659–704.

Rosenshine, B. (1983). Teaching functions in instructional programs. *Elementary School Journal, 83*(4), 335–351.

Rosenthal, R., & Jacobson, L. (1968). *Pygmalion in the classroom*. New York: Holt, Rinehart and Winston.

Rowe, M. B. (1974). Relation of wait-time and rewards to the development of language, logic, and fate control: Part II — Rewards. *Journal of Research in Science Teaching, 11*(4), 291–308.

Schwab, J. J. (1960). What do scientists do? *Behavioral Science, 5*(1), 1–27. (Reprinted in Schwab, 1978).

Schwab, J. J. (1962). The concept of the structure of a discipline. *Educational Record, 43*, 197–205. (Reprinted in Schwab, 1978).

Schwab, J. J. (1978). *Science, curriculum, and liberal education* (selected essays). Chicago: University of Chicago Press.

Schwab, J. J. (1983). The practical 4: Something for curriculum professors to do. *Curriculum Inquiry, 13*(3), 239–265.

Shavelson, R. J. (1973). What is *the* basic teaching skill? *Journal of Teacher Education, 24*(2), 144–151.

Shavelson, R. J. (1983). Review of research on teachers' pedagogical judgements, plans and decisions. *Elementary School Journal, 83*(4), 392–413.

Shroyer, J. C. (1981). *Critical moments in the teaching of mathematics: What makes teaching difficult?* Unpublished doctoral dissertation, Michigan State University, East Lansing.

Shulman, L. S. (1983). Autonomy and obligation: The remote control of teaching. In L. S. Shulman & G. Sykes (Eds.), *Handbook of teaching and policy* (pp. 484–504). New York: Longman.

Shulman, L. S. (1984a). The missing paradigm in research on teaching. Lecture presented at the Research and Development Center for Teacher Education, Austin, TX.

Shulman, L. S. (1984b). The practical and the eclectic: A deliberation on teaching and educational research. *Curriculum Inquiry, 14*(2), 183–200.

Shulman, L. S., & Elstein, A. S. (1975). Studies of problem solving, judgement, and decision making: Implications for educational research. In F. N. Kerlinger (Ed.), *Review of research in education* (Vol 3). Itasca, IL: F. E. Peacock.

Shulman, L. S., Sykes, G., & Phillips, D. (1983, November). *Knowledge growth in a profession: The development of knowledge in teaching.* Proposal submitted to the Spencer Foundation, Stanford University School of Education, Stanford, CA.

Simon, H. A. (1957). *Models of man: Social and rational: Mathematical essays.* New York: John Wiley.

Smith, B. O. (1983). Some comments on educational research in the twentieth century. *Elementary School Journal, 83*(4), 488–492.

Smith, L. H., & Geoffrey, W. (1968). *The complexities of an urban classroom: An analysis toward a general theory of teaching.* New York: Holt, Reinhart and Winston.

Soar, R. S., & Soar, R. M. (1979). Emotional climate and management. In P. L. Peterson & H. J. Walberg (Eds.), *Research on teaching.* Berkeley CA: McCutchan.

Soltis, J. (1975). Philosophy of education: Retrospect and prospect. *Education Theory, 25*(3), 211–222.

Stallings, J. A., & Kaskowitz, D. (1974). Follow through classroom observation evaluation. 1972–73. Menlo Park, CA: Stanford Research Institute.

Toulmin, S. E., (1961). *Foresight and understanding: An enquiry into the aims of science.* Bloomington, IN: Indiana University press.

Travers, R. M. W. (Ed.). (1973). *Second handbook of research on teaching,* Chicago: Rand McNally.

Tversky, A., & Kahneman, D. (1974). Judgement under uncertainty: Heuristics and biases. *Science, 185,* 1124–1131.

Weinstein, R. S. (1983). Student preceptions of schooling. *Elementary School Journal, 83*(4). 287–312.

Winne, P. H., & Marx, R. W. (1982). Students' and teachers' views of thinking processes for classroom learning. *Elementary School Journal, 82*(5), 493–518.

Wolcott, H. F. (1973). *The man in the principal's office.* New York: Holt, Rinehart and Winston.

Yinger, R. (1977). *A study of teacher planning: Description and theory development using ethnographic and informal processing methods.* Unpublished doctoral dissertation, Michigan State University, East Lansing.

Zeichner, K. M. (1983). Alternative paradigms of teacher education. *Journal of Teacher Education, 34*(3), 3-9.

Zumwalt, K. K. (1982). Research on teaching: Implications for teacher education. In A. Lieberman and M. W. McLaughlin (Eds.), *Policy making in education. Eight-first yearbook of the National Society for the Study of Education.* Chicago: University of Chicago Press.

INDEX

N

Natural science models, 74–76
Newell, A., 56
Newtonian view of scientific progress, 76–77
Nisbett, R. E., 81
Normative conception of effectiveness, 69–70

O

Origin of Intelligence in Children (Piaget), 56

P

Paradigms
    defined, 2, 4–6
    general conception of, 4–10
    See also Research programs
Participant attributes, 13, 15
Participants, 12, 15
Pedagogical knowledge, 63
Peshkin, A., 42
Peterson, P. L., 41, 59
Phillips, D., 64
Phillips, S. U., 42
Piaget, J., 56
Plans and the Structure of Behavior (Miller et al.), 52–53, 56
Positivistic perspective, 14, 15, 74–78
Pragmatic conceptions of effectiveness, 69
Presage-context-process-product model, 8–10, 29
Prewitt, K., 78
Pribram, K. H., 52–53
Principles, knowledge of rules of, 78–80
Procedural protocols, 68
Process-product research, 7–8, 17–30, 71–72
Pygmalion in the Classroom (Rosenthal and Jacobson), 21

R

Reader, G. G., 73
Research perspectives, 14, 15
Research programs
    contrasting conceptions of effectiveness and, 69–71

general conception of, 4–10
grand strategy and, 81–84
hybrid, 3, 6–7, 10, 84
ideology and, 71–73
knowledge types produced by, 67–69
major, 17–67
vs. paradigms, 2
scientific progress conceptions and, 76–78
social science conceptions and, 73–76
synoptic map, 10–16
teacher education and, 78–81
Resnick, L. B., 60
Rosenshine, B., 18, 33, 68, 69, 79
Rosenthal, R., 21
Ross, L., 81
Rowe, M. B., 28

S

Sanford, J., 18
Schwab, J. J., 6, 14, 67, 78, 81–82
"Scientific Basis of the Art of Teaching" (Gage), 72
Scientific progress, conceptions of, 76–78
Shavelson, R. J., 56, 57, 59
Shroyer, J. C., 59
Shulman, L. S., 56–58, 63, 64, 69, 72, 83
Simon, H. A., 39, 56
Smith, B. O., 14
Smith, D., 61
Smith, E., 61
Smith, L. H., 42, 68
Soar, R. M., 17
Soar, R. S., 17
Social mediation research, 28, 36–41
Social science, conceptions of, 73–76
Soltis, J., 80
Sprafka, S. A., 58
Stallings, J. A., 18
Stevens, R. J., 18, 33, 68, 69, 79
Structure of Scientific Revolutions (Kuhn), 2
Student mediation researches, 27–28, 35–41
Study of Teaching, The (Dunkin and Biddle), 5, 8–10, 28–29